STRATEGIC PLANNING

A How-To-Do-It Manual
for Librarians

M.E.L. JACOB

*HOW-TO-DO-IT MANUALS
FOR LIBRARIES*
Number 9

Series Editor: Bill Katz

NEAL-SCHUMAN PUBLISHERS, INC.
New York, London   1990

Published by Neal-Schuman Publishers, Inc.
23 Leonard Street
New York, NY 10013

Copyright © 1990 by Neal-Schuman Publishers, Inc.

All rights reserved. Reproduction of this book, in whole or in part, without written permission of the publisher is prohibited.

Printed and bound in the United States of America

Library of Congress Cataloging-in-Publication Data

Jacob, M.E.L.
    Strategic planning : a how-to-do-it manual for librarians / M.E.L. Jacob.
        p. cm. — (How-to-do-it manuals for libraries ; no. 9)
    Includes bibliographical references and index.
    ISBN 1-55570-074-8
    1. Library planning—Handbooks, manuals, etc. 2. Strategic planning—Handbooks, manuals, etc. I. Title. II. Series.
Z679.5.J3   1990
025.1—dc20
                                                      90-6568
                                                        CIP

CONTENTS

	List of Figures	v
	Preface	vii
1	Why Plan?	1
2	Perspective on Planning	3
	Business Planning	3
	Library Planning	4
	Summary	8
3	The Strategic Planning Process	9
	Participation	9
	Process Model	13
	Process Plan	15
	Summary	23
4	Institution and Community	25
	Advisory Committees	26
	Community Support	28
	Summary	29
5	Assumptions	31
	Explicit Listing	31
	Techniques	33
	Summary	34
6	Environmental Scanning	39
	Scenarios	39
	Environmental Assessment	47
	Institution Assessment	54
	Library Assessment	55
	Summary	59
7	Strategic Focus	61
	Vision	61
	Mission	61
	Goals	64
	Objectives	65

	Action Plans	67
	Policies and Procedures	72
	Summary	73
8	Values, Priorities, and Resources	75
	Values	75
	Value-added Services	77
	Priorities	82
	Resource Allocation	85
	Summary	86
9	Plan Format and Communication	89
	Audience and Message	89
	How to Communicate	93
	When to Communicate	98
	Resources	98
	Summary	99
10	Monitoring and Evaluating	101
	Plan Monitoring	101
	Monitoring the Environment	103
	Summary	105
11	End Note	107
	Appendix A. Market Research Firms	111
	Appendix B. Library Futures	113
	Strategic Planning Glossary	115
	Bibliography	117
	Index	119

LIST OF FIGURES

3-1   Participation in Decision Making
3-2   Planning Process Model
3-3   Planning Overview Statement Checklist
3-4   Planning the Strategic Plan Workform
4-1   Linkage Checklist
5-1   Sample Strategic Scenario Assumptions
5-2   Assumptions Workform
6-1   Environmental Trends Workform
6-2   OCLC Environmental Trends Extract
6-3   Thomas Jefferson University Library Environmental Trends Extract
6-4   OCLC Environmental Tracking Report Extract
6-5   Scenario Matrix
6-6   Information Industry Association Future Scenarios
6-7   OCLC Scenarios
6-8   Scenario Workform
6-9   Environmental Trends Checklist
6-10 Institutional Assessment Workform
6-11 Library Assessment Workform
7-1   Strategic Focus Overview
7-2   Mission Statement Workform
7-3   Goals Workform
7-4   Objectives Workform
7-5   Rebecca Crown Library, Rosary College, Action Plan Extract
7-6   Umpqua Community College Library Long-Range Plan Extract
7-7   Action Plans Workform
8-1   Values Overview
8-2   Value-added Manufacturing
8-3   Robert Taylor's Model of Value-added Information Services
8-4   Value-added Services in Publishing
8-5   Value-added Library Services
8-6   Simplified Model of Activity/Budget Requirements
9-1   Communications Plan Checklist
9-2   Strategic Plan Outline
9-3   AT&T Bell Libraries Mission Statement
9-4   OCLC Strategic Planning Brochure
9-5   Las Vegas Clark County Public Library Strategic Plan Brochure
10-1 Gross Unit Cost Example
11-1 Strategic Planning Checklist

PREFACE

While all organizations can use the basic principles of strategic planning outlined in this manual, the book is intended primarily for smaller institutions. It is a practical how-to-do-it manual with checklists, workforms, and samples. Not an academic treatise on planning, the book draws on over 25 years of practical experience with public, academic, and special libraries. Much of the material has been used with the Association of College and Research Libraries continuing education workshops and has been refined by reviewing and analyzing the planning documents of over 200 OCLC member libraries. Most of it consists of common sense and good management practice. Many library managers are already using some of these techniques in managing their libraries. The models and scenarios may, however, contain some new elements. Hopefully, this manual will provide the impetus to integrate and use these techniques as a regular part of planning.

This is a hands-on manual. Therefore, readers should feel free to duplicate the forms and use them to create a planning workbook. Moreover, the text outlines the pitfalls and how to avoid them. Librarians can also use these same techniques in planning and managing their careers and personal lives. This book contains all the tools needed to plan and to manage growth and change in a library.

1 WHY PLAN?

Strategic planning is a time-consuming process. So why should libraries, which are already overburdened and underfunded, take on yet another task? Strategic planning can help such libraries to best use the resources they already have. Libraries must rethink their roles and the services they provide, if they expect to continue operating. In order to survive and flourish, they need tools to make the difficult decision of where they can best spend the resources they have. Equally important, they must identify the resources they need to improve their services and they must determine where and how to obtain these resources. A strategic planning process can provide focus, mobilize support, and assist a library in identifying and tapping new resources.

Most management writers explicitly include either planning or setting objectives as an essential management function. In 1937, Gutlick enumerated the traditional management functions, which included: planning, organizing, staffing, directing, coordinating, reporting and budgeting.[1] In 1979, Zaltmon in *Management Principles for Nonprofit Agencies and Organizations* reduced these to planning, organizing and controlling.[2] While planning is part of daily management, what is strategic planning and strategic management? What does strategic mean? Can using strategic planning techniques make a difference?

> Strategic planning focuses on the vision of what a library or institution desires to be:
>
> Where a library is going
> How it will get there
> Which obstacles it should avoid
> How it can effectively meet its community's needs

It encompasses the present decisions and actions that must occur to make that vision a reality. It is a process aimed at maintaining the balance of focused commitments and resource flexibility. Strategic planning creates a framework in which knowledgeable decisions can be made based on the analysis of an institution's past, present, and anticipated future performance, and uses the results of present actions and environmental trends as guides to modifying present actions. In this way, the process determines and maintains the relationship of the institution to its environment through objectives and resource allocations targeted to achieve those objectives.

Strategic planning focuses on what an institution intends to accomplish within a five- or ten-year timeframe and broadly how it expects to reach its objective. Strategic management is the process of making and implementing decisions consistent with the library's goals as identified in the long-term strategic plan. Strategic planning provides the framework within which strategic management operates. Tactics focus on the near-term steps required to implement strategy. Strategic management uses tactics to implement strategic planning. Thus while both strategic planning and strategic management are future oriented, they recognize that actions take place in the present.

A strategic plan can provide a rallying point for library staff, for clientele, for funders, for parent institution administrators and for library supporters. It can be used to turn enemies into friends. It can improve staff morale and commitment. By bringing people together and involving them in working toward common goals, strategic planning can accomplish what seem to be miracles.

This workbook describes the process of strategic planning and provides simple tools and techniques to implement the process. The main requirements are energy, enthusiasm, commitment and leadership. Without these, the most sophisticated tools are useless. With them, even poor tools can produce useful results. And with good tools, you can achieve superior results. The objective of these tools is to unleash the creativity of your staff and to channel that creativity into productive action, which is really what strategic planning is all about.

The next chapter was written for readers who are interested in the history of strategic planning and first describes its use and development in the business community and then discusses its use in libraries. Readers who are more nuts-and-bolts oriented may want to skip to Chapter 3.

REFERENCES

1. Luther Gutlick and Lydall Urwick, ed., *Notes on the Theory of Organizations*. Papers on the Science of Administration (New York: Institute of Public Administration, 1937): p.13.
2. Gerald Zaltmon, ed., *Management Principles for Nonprofit Agencies and Organizations*. (New York: Amacom, 1979).

2 PERSPECTIVE ON PLANNING

Business Planning
Library Planning
  Federal Initiatives
    LSCA
    National Commission on Libraries and Information Science
    Library of Congress
    National Library of Medicine
    National Agriculture Library
  State Libraries and State Agencies
    U.S. Department of Education
    Massachusetts, California, Florida, Michigan
  Professional Associations
    Public Library Association
    Association of Research Libraries
    Other Initiatives
  Networks and Cooperatives
    OCLC
    WLN, RLG
Summary

Planning is not new. The ability to anticipate and plan for the future was first a survival tactic. In order to survive harsh winters, early people living in northern climates had to plan. Early farmers had to decide in advance when to plant and how to use their harvest. Pastoralists planned the use of pastures and grazing lands, stock blood lines, and the culling of flocks and herds. The use and development of military strategy are well documented. Later, planning became an economic advantage. For example, merchants had to anticipate demand in order to price their goods.

To understand library planning, an examination of the evolution of business planning is essential. While business planning has been performed throughout human history, strategic business planning in its present form is largely a twentieth century phenomenon.

BUSINESS PLANNING

As a business activity, planning evolved out of a general emphasis on planning in the United States. This emphasis was spurred by the use of planning techniques during World War II and by the economic growth following the war. Two types of planning were used: program planning and budgeting (PPB), and the Harvard Business School's method of emphasizing overall corporate strategy.[1]

Relying on formal processes to control operations, PPB extended annual budgets to five-year forecasts in recognition that financial consequences of decisions were often long-term. In capital-intensive industries such as power plant construction and communication systems, the costs were high and the return on investment could stretch out over a twenty-five year period.

Harvard stressed the different functions of an organization and viewed production, finance and marketing as separate functions with their own set of procedures and concepts. Strategic planning was one way to integrate these separate functions into a corporate entity with common goals.

Like so many management techniques, interest in planning and planning techniques has waxed and waned.[2] Planning articles began to appear in the late fifties. By the sixties, strategic planning had become a routine business function. During the recession of the 1970-71, some disenchantment set in, and by the early eighties other techniques claimed management's attention, including quality circles, corporate culture and portfolio management. Michael Porter, a noted scholar of corporate planning, criticized strategic planning efforts as failing to inculcate strategic thinking.[3]

The present business environment has moved away from the large centralized, corporate staff planning offices of the seventies to a decentralized process that places much of the planning responsibilities on line managers. One reason for this change was to ensure that planning meshed with the daily operations of the company and also to ensure that those planning were the same persons responsible and accountable for implementation of the plan. Repeatedly criticized for focusing on short-term gains at the expense of long-term investment, business managers are still trying to solve the problem of linking reward systems with long-term performance.

LIBRARY PLANNING

Librarians began to employ planning processes in the late sixties. The number of articles and books on the use of planning techniques for libraries grew steadily during the late seventies and early eighties. As a result of initiatives such as California's Proposition 13 and Massachusetts' 2 1/2, which reduced resources for some publicly funded libraries, librarians had to document their needs for resources to parent institutions and funding agencies and demonstrate that they could manage resources effectively. Concurrent with increasingly scarce public funds and foundation funds diverted to other social needs, colleges and universities emerged from a growth period to face high inflation, reduced enrollments due to demographic changes, and deteriorating physical plants and research facilities. Out of economic necessity, these institutions and their libraries increased the use of planning. For academic libraries a further impetus was the rapidly rising serial prices of the late eighties. Automation and the use of technology spurred others to planning activities. Finally, a number of organizations and funding agencies have encouraged the use of planning as a tool for library administration: federal initiatives, state libraries and library agencies, professional library associations and networks.

Federal Initiatives

Funding agencies at the federal level have had far-reaching effect in promoting the use of planning by libraries. Perhaps the most significant federal initiative has been the Library Services and Construction Act (LSCA). Passed in 1956, the Library Services and Construction Act was amended in 1966 to require a five-year state plan. The 1984 reauthorization of LSCA reasserted the requirement for statewide planning and provided specific elements to consider in the development of plans for state interlibrary cooperative relations and networking. Currently, all states have developed five-year plans and have filed them with the United States Office of Education to meet the requirements for federal funding under LSCA.

In 1976, the National Commission on Libraries and Information Science (NCLIS) developed its planning document, "Toward a National Program for Library and Information Services: Goals for Action." In 1979 the White House Conference on Library and Information Services followed. Legislation for a second conference was signed in August 1988. A number of state conferences preceded the 1979 Conference, which has been followed since by a tracking process to monitor state action on resolutions from the 1979 Conference. The resolutions have influenced both the LSCA program and state planning initiatives.

The Library of Congress (LC) has been reviewing its structure and functions. As a result, LC began an extensive planning process, which is likely to have far-reaching effects on libraries and information services. LC creates and distributes MARC, machine-readable cataloging records, and maintains the LC Subject Headings and Classification Schedules and the Dewey Decimal Classification Schedules. Its Names and Series Authorities are important to many libraries. Any changes will affect the library and information services communities.

The National Library of Medicine has sponsored the Integrated Automated Information Management Systems program (IAIMS) since 1983. In her 1982 landmark report, "Academic Information in the Academic Health Sciences Center: Roles for the Library in Information Management," Nina Matheson proposed the conceptual basis for this program, which focused on integrating advanced medical center information systems into a campus-wide information system for major universities' campuses.[4] The National Library of Medicine has funded a series of IAIMS planning and implementation grants to major educational institutions. These plans call for access to office automation, hospital and patient records, and library resources through the use of integrated, automated information systems.

In 1985, the NLM Board of Regents commenced a long-range planning process for NLM. Initial reports were published in 1986 and 1987, and the process will continue, as will IAIMS, to influence planning in the health sciences libraries.[5]

More recently the National Agriculture Library has undertaken cooperative shared cataloging programs and created a network to share resources and plan for the future of agricultural information services. USAIN, the U.S. Agriculture Information Network, was established in 1989 with Nancy Eaton as its president.

State Libraries and State Agencies

As noted above, the LSCA legislation and the White House Conference both influenced state planning efforts. In the early seventies, the U.S. Department of Education provided assistance to the Ohio State University Evaluation Center to train state library staff in using planning processes and to assist in developing long-range plans. In 1976, a follow-up session was held in Washington, D.C. and at the University of Pittsburgh. Present LSCA legislation requires five-year plans for state agencies seeking funding of certain projects under LSCA authorization.

Some states have also developed programs and documents to assist libraries with planning. For example, Nancy Bolt and Corine Johnson developed a manual for use by small Massachusetts public libraries.[6] Active under Gary Strong, California has held several conferences involving business, community leaders, educators, librarians and legislators. Jim Fry in Michigan and Barrett Wilkins in Florida have led planning efforts for state library services in their states and have developed written plans.

Professional Associations

Professional associations have been actively using planning techniques for their own operation and have encouraged use of such techniques by their members. Perhaps foremost in this regard has been the Public Library Association (PLA), a division of the American Library Association. Under the leadership of Nancy Bolt, the PLA has supported and published *Planning Process,* a publication that helps public libraries with a step-by-step approach to developing a long-range plan.[7] With the objective of creating products to expand existing use by the public libraries of planning and performance measures, PLA has participated in funding the Public Library Development Program in conjunction with the Chief Officers of State Library Agencies (COSLA) and the Urban Libraries Council.

The Association of Research Libraries (ARL) instituted a program of self-study for member libraries, with a rigorous multi-year internal analysis and planning process. After training by ARL staff, a number of major ARL libraries executed the self-study during the early eighties. ARL has published a Spec Kit, Number 108, devoted to strategic planning in its member libraries.[8]

The American Library Association, the Association of College and Research Libraries, the Medical Library Association, and the Special Libraries Association have all undertaken planning processes. They have also, through their continuing education programs, provided training in strategic planning for their members and others attending their courses.

Networks and Cooperatives

Like most organizations, networks and bibliographic cooperatives have also turned to strategic planning to better cope with change and with increased uncertainty. *Planning in OCLC Member Libraries* provides a description of planning in OCLC, in regional networks and in its member libraries.[9] In addition, the publication provides examples of OCLC planning documents, a fairly detailed description of the process as it was in 1988 and brief summaries of network plans.

With a new president in 1981, OCLC reviewed its planning process and instituted a new strategic planning process in 1984. Over the following years, OCLC discussed with its Users Council many aspects of its strategic plan, particularly its environmental tracking activities. In 1987 it undertook with the Users Council a survey of its member libraries. Over 2200 responded, and several hundred sent copies of planning documents to OCLC.

The other cooperatives, Western Library Network and the Research Libraries Group, have also undertaken strategic planning. Although they have not made the details of their efforts as widely available as OCLC has, the Research Libraries Group did provide a printed brochure on its major strategic goals.

The OCLC survey, one of the most extensive undertaken on planning in libraries, clearly demonstrates that libraries are indeed using planning generally, and strategic planning in particular.

SUMMARY

Planning has been part of human activity for most of history. Strategic planning for a long time was considered primarily a military concern until its widespread adoption and use by the business community during the sixties. The application of strategic planning techniques in libraries has followed and paralleled that in business. National, state, and professional association activities have strongly encouraged it. In some environments, parent institutions, accreditation agencies, or governmental bodies have mandated it. The next chapter will explore the strategic planning process and its adaptation to libraries.

REFERENCES

1. Michael Porter, "Corporate Strategy: the State of Strategic Thinking," *The Economist* 17: (May 23, 1987).
2. Richard F. Vancil, *Harvard Business Review: Planning Series,* Part IV, 7054: 1.
3. Porter, "Corporate Strategy."
4. Nina Matheson and John A.D. Cooper, "Academic Information in the Academic Health Sciences Center: Roles for the Library in Information Management," *Journal of Medical Education* 57 (10), Part 2 (October 1982).
5. National Library of Medicine, "Long Range Plan," (Washington, D.C.: U.S. Department of Health and Human Services, December 1986 and January 1987).
6. Nancy Bolt and Corine Johnson, *Options for Small Public Libraries in Massachusetts: a Planning Guide* (Chicago: Public Library Association, September 1985).
7. Charles R. McClure et al., *Planning & Role Setting for Public Libraries: a Manual for Options and Procedures* (Chicago: American Library Association, 1987).
8. *Strategic Planning in ARL Libraries.* ARL Spec Kit #108. (Washington, D.C.: Association of Research Libraries, Office of Management Studies, 1984).
9. M.E.L. Jacob, ed. *Planning in OCLC Member Libraries,* (Dublin, Ohio: OCLC, 1988).

3 THE STRATEGIC PLANNING PROCESS

Participation
   Advisory Committees
   Staff
   Community
Process Model
   Situation Analysis
   Strategic Focus
   Implementation
Process Plan
   Planning Rationale
   Objectives
   Scope
   Participation
   Data Gathering
   Results
   Resources
   Process and Schedules
Summary

Strategic planning is a process, not the creation of formal documents. Ideally, it is a way of thinking that should pervade all decision making within the library. It enables an organization to understand and share a common vision and common set of values and, as Peter Drucker has said, to better assess "the futurity of present decisions."[1] By having a vision of the future in mind and having assessed the various actions for accomplishing that vision, individual staff can more appropriately make day-to-day decisions compatible with achieving that desired state. They can manage strategically.

In developing a strategic planning process, planners must consider a number of key variables:

    Underlying assumptions
    The current and future state of the environment
    The state of the library and its parent institution
    Institutional, library and personal ambitions
    Leadership
    Participation

Various aspects of each of these will be discussed at some length, starting with the key question of who should participate in the planning process. The answer is: everyone who will be affected or who may be essential to achieving the vision identified in the plan. Often this is easier to define in retrospect than in prospect.

PARTICIPATION

In gathering information, broad participation is essential. When making the final and difficult decisions, the participation narrows down to a very few. As implementation proceeds, however, it again broadens out. As Figure 3-1 indicates, the results of the process are shaped like an hourglass. Broad participation at key points in the process also ensures commitment to achieving the vision identified and organizational adherence to the values enumerated.

Libraries and information centers will vary in structure, institutional relationships, governance, and environments. For example, public libraries and publicly funded academic institutions may have restrictions imposed by state agencies and by boards of

10 STRATEGIC PLANNING

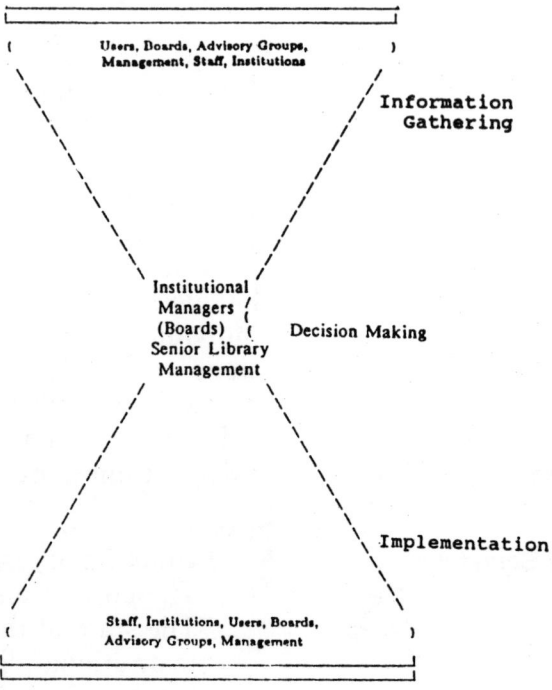

FIGURE 3-1

trustees, while corporate libraries may only be responsible to company management. Since institutional participation and commitment are essential, representation from those to whom the library reports should be encouraged. Such participation becomes critical when seeking resources or changes in regulations or policies to accomplish the library's strategic vision.

Advisory Committees

Most libraries have user groups such as a Friends' group, a faculty committee, or other advisory body. The participation of members of advisory bodies, such as influential citizens, business leaders, or faculty can help to influence the institution and its resource allocation process. Thus, the strategic planning process should encourage involvement and participation by these groups. Most of these groups have been formed to inform and support the library. They have much to contribute, and their input is essential to a successful planning process.

Staff

Staff participation is another critical element. The day-to-day operation of the library and hence the actual implementation of the planning objectives will ultimately rest on the staff's shoulders. To ensure staff commitment to the plan vision, values, and goals, managers should encourage staff to provide input and to participate in the planning process. Broad staff participation will promote a sense of ownership of the results. Direct staff involvement will generate a greater commitment to the process.

While in a large library it may be difficult to involve all staff equally, representatives of all levels can be involved. Moreover, regular communication to all staff members about progress and the proposed content of the plan can help. Participation should not be limited solely to department heads or to professional staff since all staff have a strong vested interest in the library's future and can contribute to make that future a reality.

One of the best ways to involve staff is to break down the plan into components and then to set up task groups to work on various parts of the plan. Each task group represents an opportunity to involve several different staff members. Planners and managers should make sure that these groups communicate with each other and freely share the results of their efforts. That way, the final set of recommendations will be consistent and will conform to the overall framework of the plan itself. Use of such groups in the specific aspects of the planning process are discussed in subsequent chapters.

In addition to providing staff participation through task groups, planning team members and unit heads should meet regularly with staff to inform them of plan progress and to seek comments and suggestions. Although newsletter articles, brochures, reports, and leaflets can be used to inform staff, unit meetings provide opportunities for questions and answers in a manageable forum. Ideally, even routine staff meetings should contain a planning update and give staff the opportunity to react to new developments and to provide input.

Meeting frequency will depend on how rapidly the planning process progresses. In light of the amount of brainstorming and information gathering that must be done early in the process, weekly meetings may be required to keep staff informed. Later, monthly meetings will probably suffice. Each manager will have to balance workloads and other commitments in order to fit such meetings into appropriate schedules. As noted above, planning updates should be included in regularly scheduled meetings whenever possible.

Most staff will judge by results, not by rhetoric. Consequently, while planners and managers cannot accept and act on all staff recommendations, they should identify some recommendations that can be implemented and acknowledge the source of such recommendations. If planners and managers choose not to act on certain recommendations, they should explain why.

Critical to any planning process is a common understanding of the institutional environment and the underlying assumptions about the library and the communities it serves. A thorough analysis of these will lead to an explicit statement of some of the constraints affecting both the library and its parent institution. While staff may recommend adding more staff or raising salaries, declining budgets may preclude implementing such recommendations in the immediate future. By separating short-term constraints from longer-term constraints, planners and managers can keep the channels of communication open and bolster staff morale. Managers may not be able to increase salaries in the short term, for example, but may be able to do so at some time in the future. By being as honest and as open as possible about what the problems are and what the plans are to resolve them, managers will involve staff and make them part of the solution. The problems are not just the managers'—they are also the library's and the staff's.

Community

Librarians must also remember that libraries are a means to an end and not the end in itself. The user is the *raison d'être* for the library and its collection and must be kept firmly in mind throughout the planning process. Collections that never circulate do not serve anyone; aggregates of information with no means of access are useless. That is not to say that items that do not circulate or are not accessible have no use, but ultimately a library's services and collections must meet the primary needs of its user community. Collection coverage and development policies are essential elements of a library's strategic plan. While significant input will come from collection development officers and collection development departments, the public services and the community served can provide valuable input on collection coverage and development policies. These policies should always reflect the library's mission to serve the user community. Planners and managers should rigorously examine activities, functions, collections, and

PARTICIPANTS IN INFORMATION GATHERING
Users
Boards
Advisory groups
Management
Staff
Institutions

PARTICIPANTS IN DECISION MAKING
Institutional managers
Boards
Senior library management

The Strategic Planning Process Model

Phase 1
Analyze current situation of the library, the parent institution and their environments
—library's and parents' strengths and weaknesses
—identify problems, needs, concerns and ambitions

Phase 2
Create vision of library's future

Phase 3
Implement plan
—translate broad goals into tangible results

services that are not focused toward their primary goals, and should discard or abandon goals they cannot justify.

For some library managers and staffs, strategic planning can be a painful process of self-discovery; for most, however, it can be a highly rewarding process of creating an exciting future. Creation is one of most satisfying of all human processes. Through strategic planning, both managers and staff members can channel their creativity and improve and strengthen the organization.

Although creating a vision is exciting, realizing that vision can be hard work. The planning process itself can provide focus and commitment, thereby making the difficult choices easier and more acceptable to the community the library serves, its parent institution and its staff. Inevitably the final results will be imperfect and reflect compromise. In the process, however, the library will have moved from a passive state to an active state. Moreover, the library will have gained greater visibility and credibility than it had in the past.

Successful strategic planning is a strongly participative process. It can mobilize interest and commitment to a shared set of goals. It can generate a stronger commitment to support the library from the community it serves and from the parent institution.

PROCESS MODEL

Many models can be used for a strategic planning process. Almost every book on strategic planning contains at least one. The purpose of a model is to aid in understanding and communicating the planning process. It may show relationships, data sources, functions, and participating groups. It does not substitute for decision making, data gathering, or analysis.

Some models, such as those developed with spreadsheet software like Lotus 1-2-3 or Supercalc and the resource allocation model described on page 84 and in Figure 8-6, can aid analysis by providing insights into the impact of change on some of the variables. Usually such models are used to analyze changes in resource levels, including funding and staffing and impact on activity levels or the reverse. Typically these models deal with only a portion of the planning process.

Planning does not necessarily start at the beginning and progress smoothly through each step to the end. It is an iterative process. As new information becomes available or as planning proceeds and

14 STRATEGIC PLANNING

FIGURE 3-2

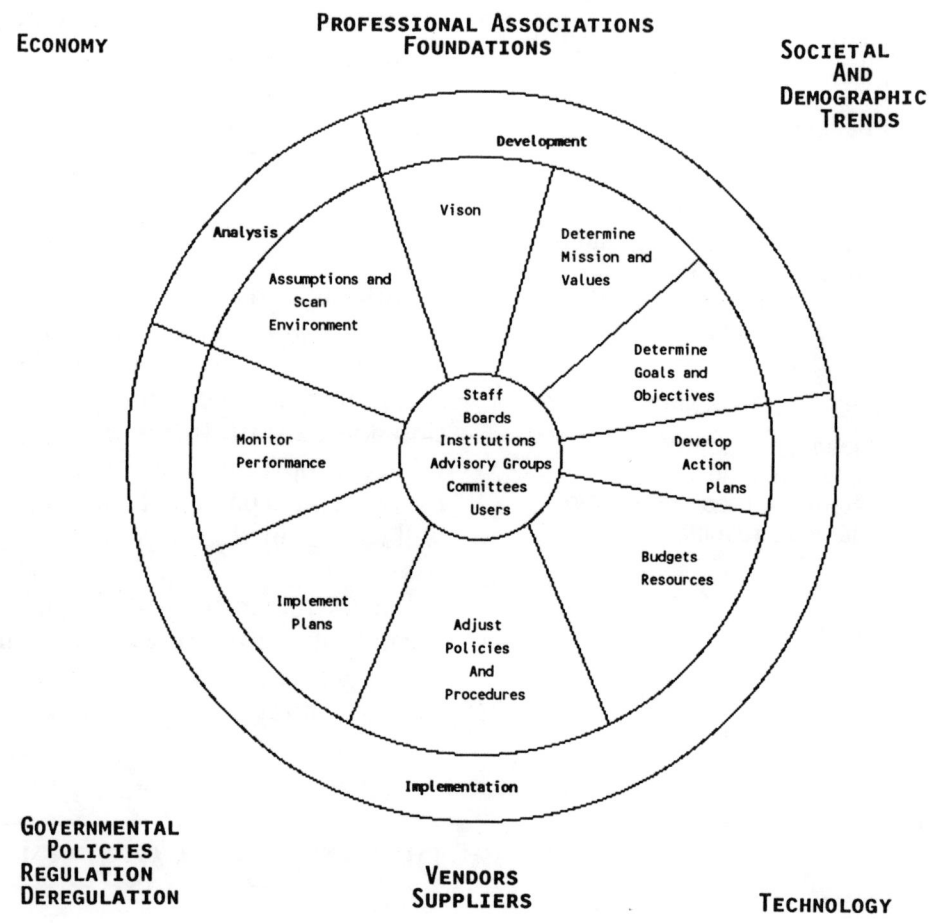

earlier data or decisions require revision or reexamination, it may be necessary to repeat steps a number of times. Figure 3-2 depicts such a conceptual model in a circular shape to illustrate that the planning process is continuous and can be entered at any stage.

The first step in developing a planning process is to do a situation analysis of the library, its parent institution and their respective environments. In the analysis phase, the planners and managers look at the library's and the parent's strengths and weaknesses and identify their ambitions, problems, needs and concerns. Typical questions to ask are:

Where are we?
What are our strengths?
What are our weaknesses?
What are key environmental trends that affect the library? Affect the library's parent?

Implementing the Strategic Planning Process

Step 1
Appoint core planning team

Step 2
Team presents staff with brief overview of plan
—Planning rationale
—Objectives
—Scope
—Participation
—Data gathering
—Results and schedules
—Resources

What is the impact of environmental trends on our strengths? On our weaknesses?
How can we maximize strengths while minimizing weaknesses?

In the second phase, the planners and managers use the results of the analysis phase to help focus on creating the type of future they desire. They should ask:

Where do we want to go?
How do we get there?

In the third phase, the planners, managers and staff implement the strategic plan by translating broad goals into concrete actions and tangible results. This phase includes communicating the plan, monitoring and reporting results, and updating the plan and its elements as needed.

There is no one best way to plan. Conceptual models such as the one presented here are merely a guide to help in understanding and may need to be modified to fit different situations. What is done at each stage will be discussed in more detail in subsequent chapters. Do note, however, that the process exists within an environment which must be understood and documented. Chapters 4, 5 and 6 discuss how this can be done.

PROCESS PLAN

The planning process normally begins with the appointment of a core planning team. The team should involve staff from all levels of the library. If time and commitment permit, the team should also include members from the institution and the community. Although planning activities initially require a considerable time commitment, they will ebb and flow later in the process depending on the pace of planning activities and the rate of activities of planning task groups.

The core team should plan to use task and work groups to complete specific tasks within the planning process. In the process, the planners and managers will have ample opportunity to involve a wide spectrum and number of both library staff and the library's community. Section 3 in Figure 3-3 offers many areas where planners can call on task and work groups to contribute.

Once the planning process is started, planners and managers can

FIGURE 3-3   PLANNING OVERVIEW STATEMENT CHECKLIST

		Chapter
1.	Statement of work	3
	Major reasons for planning	
	Accreditation	
	Institutional initiative	
	External agency initiative	
	Board initiative	
	Advisory committee initiative	
	Library management initiative	
	General aims and objectives	
	Broad vision of library in future	
	Library clientele	
	Library services	
	Scope of plan	
	Library strategic plan	
	Unit strategic plan	
	Functional area plan	
	Linkages with institution (library, unit, other functions)	
	Anticipated time frame (5, 8, 10 years)	
2.	Plan of work	3
	Phases	
	Analysis	4-6
	Plan development	7
	Plan implementation	10
	Participants	3
	Core planning team	

FIGURE 3-3 *Continued*

>>> Others that managers believe should be used on task teams

>> Anticipated Methods 6

>>> Literature searches

>>> Surveys

>>> Consultants or contractors

>>> Meetings

>>> Task forces

> 3. Possible project results (This can be specified after as part of the team's first report with their projected planning schedule)

>> Interim reports

>>> Preliminary report on schedule and structure for planning process 3

>>> List of assumptions 5

>>> Library assessment 6

>>>> Strengths

>>>> Weaknesses

>>>> Threats

>>>> Opportunities

>>>> Ambitions

>>>> Clientele

>>>> Services

>>>> Clientele needs

>>> Institution assessment 6

>>>> Strengths

>>>> Weaknesses

>>>> Threats

FIGURE 3-3 *Continued*

	CHAPTER
Opportunities	
Ambitions	
Needs	
Environmental trends	6
Scenarios	6
Draft vision statement, mission statement	7
Draft goals	7
Draft objectives	7
Preliminary resources plan	8
Draft implementation schedule	10
Final plan	9
Action plans	7
Resource plans	8
Communication plan	9
Implementation schedule	10
Maintenance plan	10

FIGURE 3-4 PLANNING THE STRATEGIC PLAN WORKFORM

1. Statement of work:
   Rationale:

   Objectives:

   Scope:

2. Plan of work
   Core planning team:

   Others:

   Methods:

3. Results | Include Yes/No | Start | Finish
   Interim reports
     Preliminary report and schedule
     List of assumptions
     Library assessment
     Institution assessment
     Environmental trends
     Scenarios
     Draft vision statement, mission
       statement
     Draft goals
     Draft objectives
     Preliminary resources plan
     Draft implementation schedule
   Final plan
   Communication plan
   Implementation schedule
   Maintenance plan

4. Resources:

present staff with a brief overview of what they anticipate doing. A checklist for the overview appears in Figure 3-3, and a workform appears in Figure 3-4. The checklist is extensive and may contain sections that do not apply to some libraries. The core planning team can use the checklist in developing its own work plan. The overview may only contain a brief paragraph on each section. In any event, managers and planners should try to keep the overview to one page if possible. The intention at this stage is not to create the final plan, but to help the core planning team to get on with its task quickly.

While this manual can serve as general background information, the one-page summary should outline:

> Major reasons for plan
> The manager's view of general aims and objectives
> Scope of functions, activities, or units to be included
> Who will participate
> What techniques and tools are to be used (this is particularly important if surveys are to be undertaken)
> What results are expected and on what schedule
> What resources will be available to the planning team including funds for literature searches, surveys or other research, secretarial support, consultants or contractors, publications, meetings, and travel

Planning Rationale

Planning processes are initiated for a variety of reasons. The parent institution may already have a planning process in place or may be responding to accreditation or governmental agency requirements for plans. Librarians may be responding to encouragement from professional associations. Alternatively, they may initiate a planning process in response to an institutional initiative or to an accreditation process. An awareness of the planning rationale may be useful to those developing the plan.

Objectives

Establishing general aims and objectives helps to direct the planning process toward specific goals. While establishing objectives can provide a useful starting point in the planning process, care should be exercised not to dictate the ultimate plan since much that is discovered during the environmental review could invalidate or modify preliminary objectives.

Scope

The scope should indicate whether the plan is for the library as a whole, for a sub-unit, or for a particular function such as collection development, technical services, or automation. It should also indicate whether plans already exist at other levels and what relationship this planning effort has with those plans.

Participation

While developing the composition of the core planning team, functional areas or titles of positions may be used. However, at the onset of the planning process, the names of the core planning team must be determined.

Planning is a team process. While a core team may coordinate the process, task forces dealing with specific aspects can be useful, both in bringing added expertise to the process and involving a larger number of people in portions of the planning activity. Once it is appointed, the core team can, as part of its planning, identify specific tasks and the expertise needed for those tasks. The team can submit an interim report with such recommendations to library management for review and approval.

Data Gathering

As discussed extensively in Chapters 4, 5 and 6, the types of data needed include:

> Assumptions
> Environmental trends
> Clientele and institutional needs
> Library and institutional strengths and weaknesses
> Opportunities for the library
> Threats to the library

At this point managers should indicate whether they will support the use of surveys and consultants, but should leave the recommendations on how best to accomplish the planning tasks to the team.

Results

Discussed extensively in Chapters 9 and 10, planning results and schedules include written statements or reports on:

> Institutional linkage (Chapter 4)
> Assumptions (Chapter 5)
> Environmental trends (Chapter 6)
> Scenarios (Chapter 6)
> Library assessment (Chapter 6)
> Plan content and format (Chapter 9)

Managers should indicate what reports (written or verbal) they expect as the planning work progresses, approximately when they want them, and how they want the processes documented. They will probably want an early report on how the team plans to proceed, its anticipated schedules and its resource requirements. Further reports on assumptions and the situation analysis are also useful. Each step of the process should result in a report, verbal or written. Such reports enable library managers to keep abreast of progress and to ensure they are comfortable both with the pace of the plan and with its proposed content.

Resources

At this early point managers may not be comfortable with establishing a planning budget and may set this as an early task for the planning team to estimate. Managers should recognize that while the process will be demanding of staff resources, they can minimize external costs by not using consultants or not engaging in extensive travel. It is possible to do planning with minimal resources. For instance, published resources can be an economical and plentiful source of data. This is discussed more fully in Chapter 6.

Process and Schedules

At this point, the managers and the planning team should be ready to begin the process. The details of what needs to be done, workforms, and checklists are included in the following chapters with a master checklist for the plan in Chapter 11. In the first step, the core planning team meets to review available materials, to clarify their understanding of the task and to prepare a list of questions, a preliminary schedule and plan for the process. The team should refine the preliminary material as they implement the planning process. The checklists in Figure 3-3 and in Chapter 11 help to define the necessary tasks.

How long will it take? That depends on the amount of data to be collected and analyzed, the number of people involved (and their personalities) and the external constraints on the schedule. A year is a reasonable amount of time, but it is possible to do a competent job in six months. If the team has less than six months, there may not be sufficient time to analyze data adequately or to use the process to change attitudes and build commitment to the plan and the planning process. If surveys and consultants are used, the process could take as long as 18 to 24 months to complete. The longer the process stretches out, the more likely it is that initial energy and enthusiasm will wane. (It is important to remember that the plan is only the beginning; plan implementation will stretch out for five to ten years.) Unless people begin to see something tangible, they lose interest and sometimes commitment. Constant reinforcement in the form of continued communication on plan progress and results is necessary. Communication processes are discussed more fully in Chapter 9.

SUMMARY

An iterative, interactive team process, planning is an ongoing way of managing and operating, not a one-time exercise. The beginning stages require broad input. During the decision-making process, the sources of input and participation narrow only to broaden again during the implementation process. Conceptual models can be useful tools in communicating what the process is, who is involved and how it works. Computer models can be useful in trying various options and assessing the likely results. The keys throughout strategic planning are gathering the essential facts, analyzing those facts and involving people at all levels. Communication is essential with staff at all levels throughout the library, with the parent institution and the communities the library serves. Finally, there is no one best process.

REFERENCES

1. Peter Ferdinand Drucker, *Management: Tasks, Responsibilities, Practices.* (New York: Harper & Row, 1974), p.125.

4 INSTITUTION AND COMMUNITY

Advisory Committees
Community Support
Summary

Few libraries exist as completely independent institutions. Most exist within another institution or report to another political unit or agency. Even the Library of Congress is responsible to a Congressional oversight committee. Consequently, the library or information center must ensure that its vision, mission, values and goals are consistent with those of its parent or governing organization.

Ideally, if the parent organization or governing body has formulated a strategic plan, the library can use this plan as a base for developing its own plan. Alternatively, if the parent organization or governing body has no plan, the library can still develop a plan by documenting its assumptions about the institutional or governing body and sharing these with appropriate administrators or officers. The library's plan can also serve as an impetus to an institution to initiate its own planning process or can help to focus an existing one. In any event, the absence of an institutional plan should not prevent the library from planning or from recognizing the linkages between the library's plan and the parent institution's activities.

Examples of circumstances in which linkage is important are:

> Annexation plans of municipalities
> Acquisitions plans of companies
> Establishment of new faculties, schools, or branch campuses.

A linkage checklist appears in Figure 4-1. Much of the process of establishing linkages centers on the plans and expectations of the parent. Identifying and documenting the assumptions associated with the parent institution is discussed more fully in Chapter 6 under institutional assessment. The linkage checklist should be used in conjunction with the institutional assessment process described in Chapter 6 and shown in Figure 6-10.

To be successful, a library must be part of the information processes and the decision-making processes within its parent institution. The further removed from these the library is, the more difficulty the library will have in commanding attention and resources. If the formal structure does not support a close relationship between the library and its parent institution, the library must build informal relationships and structures that keep it informed and involved in activities important to the institution. The manager can use the strategic planning process as a valuable tool to promote this participation by the library.

KEYS TO ACQUIRING INSTITUTIONAL AND COMMUNITY SUPPORT
Consultation
Participation
Communication

ADVISORY COMMITTEES

A library committee or advisory committee should be used to involve key officials, institutional opinion leaders and community leaders. This committee can help formulate realistic goals related to the needs of the institution. More importantly, the committee can influence the parent institution to provide the resources needed to implement the plan. In some settings, the participation of significant donors and community leaders would be important.

Most libraries already have an advisory committee. If the library does not already have a committee, the library director should establish one early in the planning process by inviting appropriate people to serve on it. Members should include opinion leaders within the primary community served and may also include institutional officers or representatives.

Membership rosters of active groups and chairpersons of committees are good sources of possible candidates. Opinion leaders from the following groups who should be considered as potential committee members include:

- Faculty and university administration officers
- Business leaders
- City officials
- Chamber of Commerce members
- Rotary Club members
- Lodge or union officials
- Professional association officers or committee personnel

Ideally the director should either know these people personally or know others who will assist in enlisting their participation.

The focus should be on persons who influence others, particularly those involved in resource allocation processes. In universities, these include key faculty. Examples in the public library area would include leading business people, politicians, the spouses of both, presidents of local colleges and universities, heads of significant institutions such as local hospitals, United Way agencies, newspaper owners and bankers.

Personal invitations should, of course, be confirmed in writing. Once such a committee is assembled, the library should publicize its existence, membership and role in the planning process.

Throughout the planning process, advisory committees should be encouraged to publicize their support of planning documents

FIGURE 4-1 LINKAGE CHECKLIST

```
Institutional mission
     Relationship of library's mission to institutional
         mission
Institutional goals
     Library goals in support of specific institutional
         goals
Demographics
New facilities or services planned
     Impact on library functions, services, need for new
         functions, services
     Impact on library facilities, need for new facilities
     Impact on library staff, need for added staff
     Impact on library's collections and information
         resources, need for enhancing collections and
         information resources
Organizational changes anticipated
     Impact on library
```

and reports as they are available. Broadly communicated, their endorsement can help apprise others, including institutional officers, of the need to provide resources to support the library's mission and goals. In addition, the use of personal contacts and relationships can do much to smooth the way for budget approval processes.

Often, the scope of linkage goes beyond the visible boundaries of the reporting structure. For example, while a public library may be a municipal or county department, it serves not only the city manager and mayor, but other departments as well. An academic library not only serves its parent institution, but may also serve related institutes, foundations and even the surrounding community. A corporate library is a resource that may also be available to subsidiaries, parent companies, or professional groups.

For some libraries, the state library agency may mandate that certain services must be provided to citizens of the state or to other libraries in order to participate in state funding. This could also include network or consortia participation. Such requirements should be reflected by linkages within or through the library's strategic plan.

COMMUNITY SUPPORT

Since libraries exist within a community, the support and participation of that community in providing library resources is essential to the long-term survival of the library. Thus, the library must be sensitive to whether the community perceives the library and its services as fulfilling the community's needs. The community should perceive the library as both relevant and essential to the community.

The library must ensure that the community understands and accepts its strategic planning process and that the community participates in the plan's development. To achieve these ends, the library must incorporate into the planning process continued communication with the community about the plan and its progress. Methods for doing this include:

- Incorporating planning information in all the regular communication channels the library uses
- Formal meetings on planning progress
- Newsletter articles, written reports, brochures, leaflets, bookmarks
- Interviews of the library director, planning team members, or participating citizens by radio, television, or newspaper reporters

Chapter 9 discusses these methods in more detail.

SUMMARY

The library and its professional staff have a significant opportunity to maintain, rebuild or improve relationships with its community through the strategic planning process, which can offer a new beginning or enhance existing strengths. The process can change the view of the business members of that community and provide access to untapped resources. The library and its staff should leverage linkages with its constituents and its reporting structure to achieve strategic planning objectives. Consultation, participation and continuous communication are powerful tools in acquiring and keeping institutional and community support.

5 ASSUMPTIONS

Explicit Listing
   Limitations and Opportunities
   Continual Validation and Questioning
Techniques
   Compilation
   Communication
Summary

One of the most critical parts of the strategic planning process is identifying and documenting assumptions about the library and its environment. Each individual operates with a personal mental model of the world that defines how things interrelate. An essential element of the strategic planning process is communication. To communicate effectively people need to use the same definitions, models and set of underlying assumptions. Identifying and documenting assumptions is an important communication tool.

EXPLICIT LISTING

Writing down assumptions provides a method for explicitly identifying, documenting and sharing assumptions. Although planners and managers should identify, document and share assumptions throughout the planning process, it is especially helpful to do so during the process of environmental scanning and evaluating alternatives.

Examples of commonly held assumptions include:

> Library services should be free.
> Parent institutional funds are the only source of library operating funds.
> No library services can be eliminated.
> Union contracts and civil service regulations limit our choices.

Limitations and Opportunities

Assumptions are two-edged: they can represent either limitations or opportunities. Michael Porter has currently been investigating national competitiveness. His research indicates that successful industries cluster in certain countries. Moreover, their success results in part from overcoming some form of competitive disadvantage. For example, Japan has experienced resource constraints such as lack of raw materials, and Italy has a restrictive labor climate. The way organizations cope with and overcome competitive disadvantages determines whether they thrive or fail.

Libraries and their parent institutions face similar challenges. They can accept the apparent limitations of their environment, or they can seek to change or eliminate such constraints. No limitation is fixed or immutable unless a person assumes that it is!

A library must strike a balance with respect to changing assumptions. On the one hand, the library should not too readily accept as immutable those assumptions that it can realistically change with action. On the other hand, a library should avoid establishing unrealistic goals that it can never achieve. Achieving this balance is one of the hardest tasks facing the planning team. While almost any single condition can be changed, a large number of changes may not be realistic or desirable. For example, a library can change its organization structure, personnel and available resources. It can even change its institutional climate and senior personnel (they may leave or be promoted) although the role of a particular unit in bringing about such changes may be problematic. In contrast, seeking to have your boss or reporting relationship changed is a questionable strategy, while seeking data and assistance in changing the boss's view may be realistic.

Continual Validation and Questioning

The failure of many planning processes results from lack of imagination and creativity. Managers and planners accept certain assumptions about the environment without sufficiently questioning those assumptions. Although everything is subject to change, those who desire change are not always the ones to initiate it. Consequently, the planning process should identify those areas most amenable to change from actions initiated by the planners. One area often considered as fixed is resources. Yet this is an area that planners often can change through their efforts. For example, managers can sometimes acquire more institutional resources or can better leverage existing institutional resources to influence others to provide additional resources. Moreover, managers can obtain resources outside of the institutional framework. Public and academic institutions have increasingly undertaken development efforts to raise funds from community, Friends groups, foundations and generous donors. Commercial organizations have been able to influence government, network, vendor or other external sources.

In contrast, certain areas are less easy to change, such as government regulation or demographics (for example, aging and geographic movements of population). Although changing government policy is possible, such change requires a long-term commitment. Short of natural or man-made disaster, the size of the aging population is immutable. Planners should direct their efforts toward areas where they can more readily effect change and where change can have a positive effect. The ability to create change requires control over those factors affecting the situation or the ability to influence those who do, and enough time to complete the change.

TECHNIQUES

Managers can employ several techniques to identify or develop a list of assumptions. Small group techniques include:

> brainstorming,
> nominal small group technique
> —assembling small groups
> —writing out ideas on small cards
> —sharing one at a time
> written lists

Whatever method is used, participants in the strategic planning process should agree upon and share a combined list of assumptions.

Compilation

When working in small groups, it is helpful to designate one person as a recorder who will write with a marker pen on a large easel pad keywords for the topics and ideas discussed. As the sheets are filled, they can be detached and taped to the walls around the room so participants can refer to them if needed. These sheets provide a record of the working group session and also provide raw material for creating a summary of the results of the discussion later.

The working group should review each assumption for its significance and its potential impact on the library. The key word is "why."

> Why does the assumption exist?
> Does the assumption really matter?
> What conditions might lead to change in the assumption?
> Is this change desirable or undesirable?
> Is the assumption favorable or unfavorable to the library?

If the assumption is unfavorable, can the condition or limitation be changed, eliminated, or moderated?

If the assumption is favorable, will it continue or can the library ensure it remains favorable?

The working group must rigorously test, question and continuously review assumptions. This will be discussed further under environmental scanning.

Communication

Once the group assembles, reviews and tests a consolidated list, the list becomes an important element of the strategic plan. This list is important in the communication and implementation process and assists non-participants to grasp quickly the mental model of the library or information center's environment. Since the list may also provide a ready source of questions, the group should share it with the community served by the library. The community's participation will ensure that the list is not myopic. Figure 5-1 provides a list of sample assumptions, and Figure 5-2 is a worksheet that can be used to list, analyze, and evaluate assumptions. It is important to remember that the group should view negative assumptions as opportunities for change—not as limitations inhibiting action.

The group should explicitly consider assumptions about the library, the parent institution and the environment with respect to its clientele, communities, competitors, functions, and services. Chapter 6 discusses environmental scanning. Once that process has been completed, the group should review and revise the initial list of assumptions.

SUMMARY

The working group must explicitly identify, document, share and revise assumptions about the library as needed. Recognizing the underlying assumptions that managers, planners, staff, institutional administrators, and library users have is essential to successful planning. Managers and planners must identify and assess the importance of differing assumptions and their impact on the library. If the assumptions are wrong, it is almost a given that plans built upon them will fail. Although everyone has assumptions, they

FIGURE 5-1 SAMPLE STRATEGIC SCENARIO ASSUMPTIONS

1. Sophisticated users, particularly professionals in business, law, medicine, science and technology, will have more choice of information services in the future and as a result will not be restricted to libraries.

2. Value-added services will be available from a variety of sources. Sophisticated users will use them and such services will increasingly consist of selected pieces of information in electronic form.

3. Commercial services, including publishers, will supply tailored services aimed at business users and science and technology professionals.

4. Archival functions will remain with libraries because commercial interests (publishers and information services) see little commercial value in such data.

5. Emphasis will be on integration of information forms (graphics, sound, animation, simulation, musical scores and maps); types (books, serials and abstracting and indexing of information); and sources (different publishers).

6. There will be more emphasis on access to information and less emphasis on ownership.

7. Users will be computer literate.

8. The qualitative analysis of information and enhanced access to specific pieces of information as opposed to the containers (_e.g._, books) will be more important.

9. Technology will continue to increase in capability and decrease in price.

FIGURE 5-2 ASSUMPTIONS WORKFORM

Assumption	Impact Positive	Impact Negative	Change Likely?	Impact

are seldom required to state them explicitly or explain why such assumptions are valid. One of the most valuable parts of the strategic planning process consists of explicitly identifying such assumptions and critically examining them.

6 ENVIRONMENTAL SCANNING

Scenarios
   Information Industry
      Association
   Association of Research
      Libraries
   OCLC
Environmental Assessment
   Scanning
   Scenario Development
Institution Assessment
Library Assessment
   Community
   Competition
   Costs and Productivity
Summary

One of the most critical elements of the strategic planning process, environmental scanning or tracking is the process of identifying both the current status of the library's environment and the trends that affect the library. As noted in the previous chapter, assumptions are part of the library's mental model and help to define its environment. Curiously, managers do not always do it and if they do, they do not document the results.

Environmental scanning consists in part of identifying and listing assumptions. These particular assumptions are external to the library and involve a broad spectrum of subjects and functions. They also have diverse effects. Included are broad trends in society, government, politics, economics, technologies, business, professions, and demography. Also included are state, regional, local and institutional trends. Figure 6-1 shows a generic workform. Figure 6-2 shows an example from OCLC. Figure 6-3 shows a library example.

As part of its strategic planning process, OCLC developed an environmental tracking process that looked quarterly at its environment to identify key changes. OCLC then assessed the degree to which these changes would confirm its strategic planning goals or require changes to them. Figure 6-4 is an extract from one of OCLC's environmental scans. Areas typically reviewed included: types of libraries (academic, public, special, state, and national); legislation and regulation; regional networks; technology; economy; professional associations; international activities; competitors; and vendors and suppliers.

SCENARIOS

Scenario development—or the "what if" process—is an outgrowth of environmental scanning. "Scenario" is defined by the *American Heritage Dictionary* as "an outline of a hypothesized chain of events." Generating a description which can take a variety of different forms, scenario development identifies what a potential future might look like. The various conditions that could result from one or more selected key factors are identified and fully described. Increased or decreased enrollments, increased or decreased numbers of school age children, shifts in population, or increased or decreased resources are a few such factors. How scenarios are developed is discussed more fully later in this chapter.

A number of organizations have used scenarios to anticipate

40 STRATEGIC PLANNING

FIGURE 6-1 ENVIRONMENTAL TRENDS WORKFORM

Factor	Trend	Effects	Comments
Economy			
Technology			
Society			
Politics			
State			
Federal			
Institution			
Libraries			

FIGURE 6-2 OCLC ENVIRONMENTAL TRENDS EXTRACT

FIVE YEAR ENVIRONMENTAL TRENDS

FACTOR	TREND	EFFECTS
Technology		
Computers	More available and more flexibility	Increased capability at lower costs
	Smaller; cheaper; greater capacity at lower cost (super computers and super micros)	More capability, more and easier use by general population with a rise in computer literacy, more decentralization, shared research centers
Software	More packages, some for libraries	Cheaper; more will use in place of central service; links to local systems, terminals; integration of graphics and text; gateways
Mass storage	Higher density; cheaper	Seen as alternative to massive central database; more data can be stored locally; CD-ROM and optical storage; higher capacity and lower costs; write once and erasable will be available
Telecommunications; Switched broad band (Fiber optics/satellite) with multi-media capability	Available by 1990s; move to digital will accelerate	AT&T pushed by competition to move more swiftly into broad band switched capability-- competitors from MCI, cable; lower cost, easier entry for new services-- opportunities for publishers, others; likelihood of educational networks
LANS	More available	Interconnection of workstations/terminals within buildings and across campuses, with gateways to local and national databases
Displays	Improved	Better quality; higher resolution graphic, less costly
Print	Improved	Lower cost; higher quality
Voice input/output	Improved	Used for some tasks and to serve the handicapped
Economics		
Constrained resources	Continue	More competition; less money for some; more emphasis on local and/or state funding, less on federal; increased emphasis on resource sharing; increased private fund-raising, grants, foundations; decline in funds affects libraries' purchasing power
Library Costs	Up	Higher level staff; higher capital investments; less for services and materials; shorter amortization periods; devaluation of the dollar; higher capital and maintenance for hardware and software
Inflation	Low to moderate	Somewhat higher costs

FIGURE 6-3 THOMAS JEFFERSON UNIVERSITY LIBRARY ENVIRONMENTAL TRENDS EXTRACT

CURRENT	TRENDS/DEVELOPMENTS	LIBRARY ASSUMPTIONS
National * Users are created for libraries instead of libraries creating their markets * Libraries set up in traditional formats-- circulation, reference, reserve, etc. * Users don't know how to use and don't support libraries * Medical School enrollment grew until 1980 **Regional/Local** * Same as national * Penn & Temple medical libraries are part of large general systems * Temple has developed bibliographic instruction programs * 1st year enrollment in Philadelphia Medical Schools rose 37% between 1965 and 1976 and then stabilized * Jefferson's Diploma School of Nursing closed * Jefferson initiated new programs in occupational therapy and physical therapy.	**National** * The country is becoming an information society: users are realizing that information is valuable. Libraries are not perceived as meeting that need, and users are turning to alternative sources, e.g. information brokerage firms * It is a national trend that use in libraries is declining * Some innovations in service are appearing such as mini-Medline, workshops on services available to users (BRS after dark), end-user searching, learning resource centers, CAI, etc. * Instructional programs are being developed * Medical school enrollments is declining * Elderly utilization of hospitals is increasing * Users have a heightened consumer awareness **Regional/Local** * Local health care institutions will seek to develop multi-institutional arrangements (affiliations, shared services, etc.) * Jefferson's College and Allied Health will experience increased enrollments and offer new programs * Use at Jefferson is increasing.	* The library must do a needs assessment of its users to determine who its user population is and what services are wanted. * Innovative services will have an impact on resources (staff, collection, space) * Outside demands on the library will increase. Skills needed to meet the needs of a changing user group will have to be developed * When the library identifies the nonlibrary user out of its user population, outreach programs will have to be considered * The library will have to evaluate existing and new services to determine what services to develop * The library will have to be more active in university and hospital activities to be able to define Services/User Mix * will have to provide information, not sources

FIGURE 6-4 OCLC ENVIRONMENTAL TRACKING REPORT EXTRACT

```
OCLC
6565 Frantz Road  Dublin, Ohio 43017-0702  (614) 764-6000  FAX (614) 764-6096
```

1988 September 19

MEMORANDUM

TO: OCLC Users Council

FROM: Debbie Rings, Information Analyst
         Office of Library Planning

SUBJECT: Environmental Tracking Report

Below is a summary of summer environmental tracking activities as well as other information that may be of interest to Users Council delegates. If you have any questions, or if you have additional information regarding these items that you would like to share with us, please feel free to contact me at (614) 764-6078, or 1-800-848-5878.

Public & State Libraries

The Nashville/Davidson County (TN) Library assumed the public records and archives functions for the metro government of Nashville. They have a new separate building for records archives storage.

The California Legislature passed, and the Governor has signed, a bill to provide $75 million in bond funds for the construction of public libraries. It now must be placed on the ballot for the general election in November.

Many state libraries have initiated telefax and/or CD-ROM projects/systems:

- Idaho State Library initiated a telefax project involving major academic and public libraries.
- Indiana State Library placed 18 telefax and 27 CD-ROM systems in the state's public libraries.
- Iowa State Library to initiate a pilot project to place full text of selected documents in the Iowa Locator (the states CD-ROM resource sharing system).
- Maryland State Library beginning a project to place telefax equipment in the state's major resource libraries. Other libraries can purchase through the state at a discounted price.
- The Mississippi Library Commission used LSCA Title III funds to place telefax equipment in five state universities. Now all eight state supported universities, the Library Commission, and the two largest public libraries have telefax equipment.
- Missouri State Library is planning to fold the Missouri Union List of Serials into the state database for eventual inclusion on CD-ROM.

A bill has been passed by the California legislature which will grant a one time, 25% tax credit to donors of computers, modems, and software to public libraries for use by patrons.

OCLC Online Computer Library Center, Inc.

National Libraries

William J. Welsh, Deputy Librarian of Congress, formally announced his retirement effective October 1988.

Telecommunications

Spain's state-run telecommunications concern, Telefonica De Espana S.A., plans more joint ventures with the Soviet Union after signing a long-term agreement to assist Soviet concerns in producing pay phones and printed circuits for telecommunications equipment. Telefonica officials stated the two parties will also discuss ventures in fiber optics, the production of radio-transmitter emergency buoys for shipping, and the marketing abroad of part of these ventures' production.

Elsevier plans to buy Springhouse Corp., a publisher of journals and books about nursing and education. Terms weren't disclosed.

MacMillan is still fighting Robert Maxwell's takeover bid.

Other

A GPO "Plan" for dissemination of government information in electronic formats was released by the Joint Committee on Printing late in June, with reactions and comments requested by mid-August.

44 STRATEGIC PLANNING

FIGURE 6-5 SCENARIO MATRIX

	TECHNOLOGY ADOPTION		
ECONOMIC CONDITIONS	Low Rate of Technology Adoption	Medium Rate of Technology Adoption	High Rate of Technology Adoption
Low Economic Conditions Inflation returns, rapid upward trend - serials prices Libraries reduce all purchases Traditional users forced to rely on libraries More libraries closed	Adoption rate slows More vendor failures Higher prices Reversion to card catalogs Data Conversion slows Limited use of CD-ROM Circulation reverts to manual Document delivery is slow Depressed economy, Low technology	Continues present trends More management users More OPACs Few card catalogs left Heavy use of CD-ROM Most use automated circulation Fax is used more for ILL Depressed economy, Medium technology	Accelerated technology use Broadband LANs widely available OPACs include non-library data Card catalogs disappear Publishers supply cataloging Publishers supply contents tables Documents communicated electronically Depressed economy, High technology
Unchanged Economy Uneven patterns of funding Some users turn to electronic services Serials prices moderate More information services place demands on budgets Some print replaced by CD-ROM	Unchanged economy, Low technology	Unchanged economy, Medium technology	Unchanged economy, High technology
Improved Economy More funds available Aggressive commercial services offer users more choices Electronic services are expanded and replace print heavily	Improved Economy, Low technology	Improved economy, Medium technology	Improved economy, High technology

FIGURE 6-6 INFORMATION INDUSTRY ASSOCIATION FUTURE SCENARIOS

FACTORS	HIGH-TECH INFORMATION SOCIETY	CREATIVE SOCIETY	THINGS BOG DOWN	1984 AND BEYOND
Overall character	Optimistic, successful booming, economy, rising consumption and productivity. Low unemployment	Optimistic, creative. Future based on learning and human development	Pessimistic, some decline. Slow growth. Information gap worsens poverty	Authoritarian, Aids epidemic, Depression
Value system	Similar to present. Achievement-oriented, bottom-line	Creative, learning society. Changed values: emphasis on cooperation. Harmony with nature, equalizing role changes for women and men	Pessimistic, achievement values dominate, but people are frustrated	Survival, control-Willingness to sacrifice freedom for the sake of order and security
Privacy	New methods, no problems	Enhanced	Scandals, abused	Irrelevant
Property rights		Redefined, cooperation	Continued gap in property rights	Irrelevant
Marketing	Global markets active, 2xGNP	Fair global, cooperative approach	Information protection. Slow growth	Information protection
Government	Little competition, less active	Active, but role undefined	Competing in information prior to reducing deficit. Strong resistance to change slows potential uses of information technology	Active, controlling high-tech
Technology	Highly developed, speech recognition	Rapid progress, dynamic speech recognition, parallel processing, networks	Slow progress, aid failures, some speech recognition	Moderate progress
Information/Service/ Products	Agents. Hypertext (Alan Kaye)	New structures	New higher taxes and information gaps	Controlled information available

future conditions based on certain specified assumptions and to choose the best course of action depending on the likelihood of a particular scenario. Battelle Memorial Institute makes extensive use of this process and offers courses in scenario development techniques. Heydinger and Zentner describe the technique as used in futures forecasting.[1] Pfeiffer discusses its use in strategic planning.[2] The Information Industry Association (IIA), OCLC, the Association of Research Libraries (ARL), and others have also applied this technique. Ideally, one or two key factors should be selected and used to develop the scenarios. As each factor is varied, the elements of the scenario are reviewed and modified based on the impact of the variable. If two key variables are used and each is evaluated at high, medium, and low levels, nine separate scenarios would result, as shown in Figure 6-5.

Information Industry Association

In 1984, the Information Industry Association commissioned the Institute for Alternative Futures to review its environment and to develop associated scenarios. Figure 6-6 shows a summary of these scenarios and their associated conditions. These scenarios operate at the societal and governmental level and identify broad trends. Few libraries or institutions have developed such broad perspectives. Most libraries tend to focus on a most likely future and develop options or alternatives within that narrower perspective. They spend most of their effort on factors more directly influenced by the library or institution. Good scenario development is a time consuming and demanding process.

Association of Research Libraries

The Association of Research Libraries has also developed some broad scenarios representing different library futures. One scenario considered was the traditional library with continued focus on ownership of traditional library materials. A second scenario described parallel development of electronic services with a focus on access for online services and ownership of more traditional materials. A third described discipline-based information services (such as are offered in many branch libraries) linked to traditional core services and focused on access instead of ownership. The fourth scenario included a fully electronic library with decentralized end-user services and broad access via online connections.

The consensus among research librarians was that the second scenario was the most likely and the most desirable. These scenarios were first considered in 1984, and Dwayne Webster, Executive Director of ARL, indicated in 1989 at the World Futures Conference in Washington, D.C. that options 3 and 4 were becoming more likely.

OCLC

In contrast to the IIA broad societal scenarios and the ARL library scenarios, OCLC focused its efforts more on the potential impact on libraries of two key variables: the adoption by libraries of technology and the economic state of libraries. An example of high technology adoption with varied economic conditions appears in Figure 6-7. A blank work sheet appears in Figure 6-8 and can be modified to suit the library.

ENVIRONMENTAL ASSESSMENT

How does one go about environmental scanning and scenario development? A library can purchase the services of a consultant or a firm specializing in these activities. While a number of firms are offering such services to businesses, few are marketing to libraries. Many of these are an outgrowth of firms specializing in market research. A selected list is given in Appendix A. Many consultants, including some library consultants, would be willing to undertake such activities. Most professional associations can supply lists of consultants serving their communities. Alternately, the library can either use the result of other libraries' or agencies' efforts, if these organizations are willing to share their data, or employ internal resources to perform these activities.

Scanning

Managers and planners pursuing the do-it-yourself route can learn how to perform an environmental assessment through courses offered by continuing education programs, particularly those of SLA and the Battelle Memorial Institute seminar. In addition, a variety of information sources such as the current professional

FIGURE 6-7 OCLC SCENARIOS

Library	Poor Economy	Unchanged Economy	Improved Economy
Users	Traditional users (for schools and publics: children), historians, arts, humanities, limited sci/tech, few businesses	Traditional users, more business use, some Sci/tech	Traditional users, moderate business, medical, law, sci/tech use depending on value-added, analysis services
Functions	Archival, popular books and journals, limited online or CD-ROM bases, mainly print materials some VCR's, CD's	Archival, moderate online services, access, document delivery, many forms of materials	Value-added information analysis, switching node. Information suppliers, all forms of materials heavy emphasis on information vs container
Resources	Limited	Moderate	Extensive
Services	Limited numbers of workstations and micros Some fee-based online searching is offered	Workstations and micros are available to library staff for many functions, to users for access to library catalogs, some micro access. Lend VCR's, CD's, software, public access data files	Broad band and LAN access to all institutions and to external services. Enhanced access and data analysis services. Library acts as advisor, switching node, and research team partner
Institutions	Some institutions and libraries close Increased pressure for consolidation	Some consolidation, use of remote access	Strong encouragement to use technology instead of people Consolidate where services can be improved, but trend is to decentralize Strong stress on end user systems and patron education
Needs	Low cost, high productivity	Controllable cost, productivity enhancement, more sophisticated software Integrated information sources	Artificial intelligence and expert systems to assist with access and information analysis

FIGURE 6-8 SCENARIO WORKFORM

| Users | Functions | Services | Resources | Institutional Impact/Relations |

AREAS OF ENVIRONMENTAL TRENDS
Economy
Technology
Society
Politics
Federal
State
Institutions
Libraries

literature is available. The December or January issues of many journals contain articles that look at the year ahead, or even several years ahead. A number of monographs have also appeared describing the future for particular types of libraries. Appendix B lists examples of these.

Other useful sources include:

>   Annual reviews
>   Census Bureau forecasts
>   Chamber of commerce publications
>   Federal, state, local, or regional agency publications
>   Trade associations (IIA, Savings and Loan Associations)
>   Professional associations
>   Banks
>   Businesses
>   Consultants

Particularly useful are publications of the state commissions on the future and of state planning agencies. Some universities teach courses on future studies and have established institutes for the future or issued publications on future trends. The manager and planner must identify sources that are relevant and useful to the library, and select those factors which are most important to the particular library.

What are some of the key variables? In a public library, key variables include areas where growth is occurring and, conversely, areas where use of library services is declining because of population shifts or changes in neighborhood composition. In special libraries, new corporate directions, acquisitions, divestitures, and research activities are relevant. In academic libraries, key variables include the parent institution's ambitions, continuing education activities, new academic disciplines or departments and institutional recruiting practices.

While Figures 6-1, 6-2, and 6-3 provide broad categories that should be considered in developing an environmental scan, Figure 6-9 provides a checklist of items that may be considered. The importance of particular items will vary depending on the nature of the institution. Managers and planners should devote their efforts to those items having the greatest potential impact on the library, but they should at least consider the others, as there is no one best way to do environmental scanning.

The library should particularly assess whether identified trends will influence library users, users' needs, institutional perspectives and resource availability. Some factors and trends will be more

FIGURE 6-9 ENVIRONMENTAL TRENDS CHECKLIST

Economics
- Rate of inflation up? down? flat?
- Likely resource availability to institution? to library?
- Status of state and local economy?
- Telecommunication charges up? down? steady?
- User fees up? down? Available to library?
- State grants such as LSCA funding?
- Taxation policies likely to affect library or available resources?

Technology
- General impact on agriculture and industry?
- Institutional use and adoption of technology?
- Computer capacity and price changes?
- Mixed media systems (graphics, sound, motion)?
- Auxiliary storage such as disc, CD-ROM, tape?
- Peripherals such as printers and scanners?
- Voice input/output systems?
- Software for library applications?
- Electronic mail systems and bulletin boards?
- Electronic publishing?
- Communication system features?
- Local area networks?
- Cellular radio (branches, bookmobiles)?
- Remote or dial-up library service capabilities?

Society
- Aging population
- Literacy changes of users? of entry level staff?
- Single heads of households
- Working parents and latch-key children
- Homeless persons
- Educational system changes

Politics
- Government regulation, laws
- Federal allocations for LSCA and libraries
- Public access to public information (Federal dissemination policies)
- Potential impact of White House Conference on Libraries and Information Science
- Intellectual property rights, patents and copyrights?
- Ownership of information
- Taxation policies on services and information products
- Federal and state information policies

Federal
- Financial support to libraries
- Federal information policies
- Federal legislation affecting library and educational services
- Federal legislation affecting key economic sectors

FIGURE 6-9 *Continued*

```
State
    Financial support for libraries
    Information policies
    Reporting and statistical requirements
    Services available to libraries
    Key personnel

Institution
    Resources
    Technology use
    Key personnel
    Institutional ambitions
    (See section on Institutional assessment)

Libraries and Professional
    Professional association position on political, societal and
        library issues
    Continuing educational programs from professional
        associations
    Trends affecting specific types of libraries (Academic,
        public, school, special, law, health sciences,
        theological, government, etc.)
```

significant than others. While general economic trends are important, it is critical to look at the specific economic trends in your area. Over the last several years different parts of the United States have been affected differently by changes in the economy. Agricultural areas may feel different pressures than industrialized or high technology areas.

Environmental scanning requires processing a lot of data, out of which managers and planners select the relevant bits. Relying on the work of others, they can significantly reduce their work. For example, managers and planners can make the work more manageable by asking small groups that are already looking at relevant literature to note pertinent factors. Environmental scanning is an important part of strategic planning and of good management practice which should be done regularly.

The Public Library Planning Process and associated publications sponsored by the Public Library Association provide detailed recommendations for conducting surveys and gathering data for public libraries as well as how to use this data in planning.[3] Some public librarians have complained that this process is too cumbersome and time consuming. In response to this problem, Nancy Bolt and Corine Johnson prepared an abbreviated version for Massachusetts small public libraries.[4]

Managers and planners must balance the relevance to the strategic planning process of data gathering against its costs. Each institution must grapple with the question of how much time and how many resources to devote to this activity. While the relationship of each library to its community is unique, similarities in relationships are plentiful. Managers and planners should use the results of surveys and research that have already been published, especially if the sources reside in or are familiar with the community and its information needs.

Managers and planners should also remember strategic planning is an iterative process. If any aspect of the mission, goals, assumptions or objectives proves invalid, managers and planners can change them so long as they also ensure changes are made as needed throughout the rest of the plan to support those new requirement. Planning is meant to provide increased flexibility, not limit it. The process should assist managers in better understanding and assessing the impacts of change on the organization. The process should not, however, control the organization.

Scenario Development

Part of the scanning process may also include the development of library scenarios. Managers and planners select the two most significant environmental factors and create a matrix similar to Figure 6-5. Then they vary each factor through poor conditions, static conditions, or improved conditions or low, medium, and high rates of change by listing the assumptions and likely conditions associated with each. Figure 6-7 shows an example of a high technology matrix under varying economic conditions and the potential impact on libraries. Having identified the assumptions associated with each set of conditions, the managers and planners look at the impact by identifying what would happen to users, library functions, library services, library resources, and the parent institution under these assumptions. While some conditions will not result in significant differences, others will. By carefully considering those with differences, the manager and planners can begin to assess which scenario works best for the library and which scenarios are most likely to occur. The manager or planner can ignore factors that have little impact or are unlikely to occur. The manager or planner should rigorously consider high risk or likely factors and prepare alternative courses of action.

Scenario development is a process which requires managers and planners to document explicit assumptions about the future and identify precisely what these assumptions would mean in relation to library functions and services. The likelihood of these assumptions must be continually tested against the environmental conditions. One possible scenario would be World War III, which in the present circumstances appears to be less likely than sporadic outbursts of local or regional conflicts. Another scenario might entail a world economic collapse, which is possible but not very likely. Examples of scenario factors closer to libraries would be the increase or decrease of institutional resources, the shifts in local populations, continued inflation, or the potential shortage of professional staff for certain categories of work.

Managers and planners who have thought about factors that relate to libraries and their potential effects, will be better able to respond if they occur; they will at the least be able to chose an acceptable course of action. Budget cuts are a contingency every library manager will probably face at some point in a professional career. Surpluses also occur, although not as frequently. By not considering alternative scenarios, a manager is likely to encounter management crises, which may not allow sufficient time to select the optimal course of action.

Environmental scanning and scenario development focus on possible futures. However, before decisions can be made on the best future course, a manager or planner must become familiar with the present state of the institution and the library by performing and documenting assessment processes for each.

INSTITUTION ASSESSMENT

If an institutional planning process is in place or if an institution has recently undergone an accreditation process, the data needed for an institutional assessment will have been developed as part of those processes. If not, the manager or planner can use the process identified in Chapter 4 for documenting assumptions. Elements considered should always relate to their implications for and effects on the library. The purpose is not to do a planning process for the parent institution, but to establish a framework for understanding how the library currently relates and should relate in the future to its parent. A workform is provided in Figure 6-10. Items to be considered include:

> Institutional mission, goals and objectives (particularly those affecting library services)
> Primary clientele
> Primary functions and services
> Institutional ambitions
> Institutional strengths
> Institutional weaknesses
> Institutional needs
> Threats to the institution (and consequently to the library)

The focus should be on brief summaries of pertinent information. The manager or planner should have completed much of assessment as described earlier in Chapter 4. To ensure that the information is complete and accurate, the manager or planner should share the assessment with institutional administrators.

LIBRARY ASSESSMENT

In performing the library assessment, the manager or planner should identify and document the current state of the library. A workform for the process appears in Figure 6-11. Depending on the library services, a separate page may be needed for library services and library costs. The assessment should answer the following questions:

> Who does the library serve?
> How does it serve these people?
> What are their needs?
> Is the library meeting these needs?
> What functions does the library perform?
> To what resources does the library have access?
> What is the library not doing that it can or should consider doing?
> What are the library's strengths?
> What are the library's weaknesses?
> Do the weaknesses represent potential opportunities?
> Can the weaknesses be overcome or minimized?
> Who are the library's competitors?

FIGURE 6-10 INSTITUTIONAL ASSESSMENT WORKFORM

```
Mission:



Goals: (Those important to or affecting the library)




Community served:




Primary function and services:



Ambitions:




Strengths:




Weaknesses:




Needs:



Threats:
```

FIGURE 6-11 LIBRARY ASSESSMENT WORKFORM

Community served:
    Who: From where:

Services provided: Usage patterns:

Community needs:

Library functions:

Resources available:

Strengths:

Weaknesses/opportunities:

Competition: Competitor strategies/goals:

Library costs/productivity:

How do they pose a threat to the library?
What are their strategies, goals and objectives?
What are the library's costs?
How productive is the library staff?

The purpose of the library assessment is to understand the library's present role. The planning process will consider future opportunities at a later stage when the library's mission and goals are defined.

Critical to understanding both the library's present and future roles are three areas: the library's clientele, the library's competitors, and the library's costs.

Community

Questions related to the identification and understanding of the library's clientele are:

Who are these people?
Where do they come from?
What do they want from the library?
What do they get from the library?
Has their usage changed and is it still changing? If so, how?

As discussed earlier in this chapter, these questions can be answered in a number of ways. Mail, telephone, or in-person surveys are common methods. Other options include focus groups (i.é., small groups of users are interviewed as a group), open meetings, advisory committees or blue ribbon panels (panels of community leaders and acknowledged experts from the library community). Managers can use published reports on similar types of clientele so long as they recognize both the similarities and differences and adjust their use accordingly.

Competition

Competition is a concept foreign to many librarians. They seldom think of themselves as competing either for their clients' attention or for resources. In recent years, however, as a result of initiatives such as California's Proposition 13, rising serial prices and corporate mergers, the library's competition with services such as fire and police protection, academic departments, and corporate units has been escalating. Although new electronic services are looming on the horizon, it may be some time before these services are broadly available to large numbers of library users. More common in the corporate environment, information brokers often supplement rather than fully replace library services. Finally, direct end-user searching of online systems has made some inroads, but in most corporate libraries search demands have increased rather than decreased, although the types of searches have become more complex. Clearly users' options will continue to increase substantially in the future.

Costs and Productivity

A third critical area in the library assessment involves thoroughly understanding the library's cost basis and productivity levels. Too few libraries really understand their costs. Sources useful in measuring and understanding costs include Rosenberg,[5] Gherman,[6] and Roberts.[7] Chapter 10 discusses some simple methods of determining these costs.

SUMMARY

There are many sources of environmental data. A major step in the environmental assessment process is to identify which sources can be most helpful and which trends are most critical. Managers and planners must understand what environmental trends affect the library, its parent institution, and the communities the library serves. To plan for the future, the manager and planner must understand the library and its parent institution: their strengths and weaknesses, threats to their success, and opportunities for them to change and grow.

Once the planning team has identified environmental trends and has completed the institution and library assessments, it should identify and summarize the most important factors. This data will form the base on which the team will build the strategic plan. Scenarios or "what if" models can be helpful in identifying the important factors.

This work should provide an understanding of the influences acting on both the institution and on the library. In addition, the opportunities that most closely fit with the library's strengths should have become apparent. The next chapter discusses another approach for identifying a desired future. Such a future must be both visionary and realistic; the environmental analysis provides the basis for identifying the possible and the most likely futures.

REFERENCES

1. Richard B. Heydinger and Rene D. Zentner, "Multiple Scenario Analysis: Introducing Uncertainty into the Planning Process," in James L. Morrison, William L. Renfro and Wayne I. Boucher, eds. "Applying Methods and Techniques of Futures Research," *New Directions for Institutional Research,* 39:10(3) (September 1983):51-68.
2. William J. Pfeiffer, Leonard D. Goodstein and Timothy M. Nolan, *Shaping Strategic Planning: Frogs, Dragons, Bees, and Turkey Tails.* (Glenview, Illinois: Scott, Foresman, 1989).
3. Charles R. McClure et al., *Planning and Role Setting for Public Libraries: A Manual of Options and Procedures.* (Chicago: American Library Association, 1987).
4. Nancy Bolt and Corine Johnson, *Options for Small Public Libraries in Massachusetts—Planning Guide.* (Chicago: American Library Association, September 1985).
5. Phillip Rosenberg, *Cost Finding for Public Libraries: A Manager's Handbook.* (Chicago: American Library Association, 1985).
6. Paul Gherman and Lynn Scott Cochrane, "Developing and Using Unit Cost: The Virginia Tech Experience." *LAMA* 3(2) (Spring 1989):93-96.
7. Stephen A. Roberts, *Cost Management for Library and Information Services* (London: Butterworth's, 1985).

7 STRATEGIC FOCUS

Vision
Mission
Goals
Objectives
Action Plans
Policies and Procedures
Summary

A strategic plan consists of a number of different elements. Elements common to all plans include a mission statement, goals, objectives and action plans. While individual plans may encompass other elements, those listed are essential. Figure 7-1 shows the relationships among these elements.

VISION

Some processes start with a vision statement which defines a future view of the library, from which a mission statement may be derived, while others start with a mission statement, which is described in the next section. A vision statement should be oriented towards the future and should be almost out of reach so that the library and its staff must stretch to reach the vision. The vision statement should reflect idealism and contain qualitative phrases. Not all writers distinguish between a vision statement and a mission statement since both contain similar elements and essentially overlap. In part, the list of assumptions discussed in Chapter 4 forms the nucleus of materials to draw upon for developing either a vision or a mission statement. A written mission statement is essential regardless of whether a library articulates a vision statement.

MISSION

One of the most important steps in the planning process is for a library or information center to define its mission. In a succinct and highly focused manner, the mission statement should:

> Identify the community or communities the library serves
> Describe the way in which it serves these communities
> Establish a vision of what the library will become
> Provide a sound base for decentralized decision making
> Stand without modification for a considerable period of time

The mission statement should clearly define what a library is and does, but at the vision level. It should not:

> Be a detailed laundry list of library services

Be a multi-paragraph, multi-page statement
Be continually modified
Reflect only today's goals

The statement should be simple and easy to understand. It should not contain too many details, which can appear in the

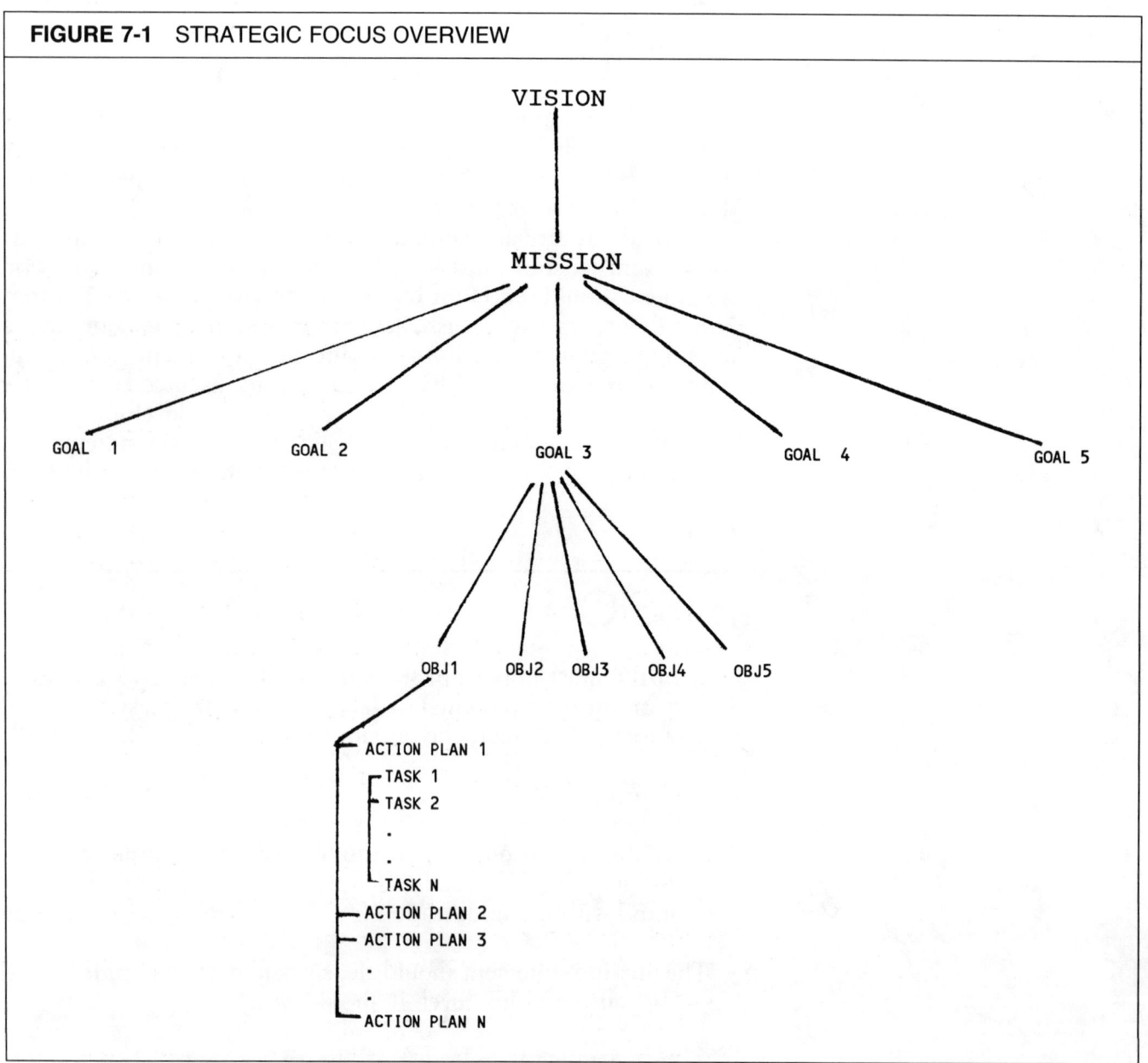

FIGURE 7-1 STRATEGIC FOCUS OVERVIEW

statement of supporting goals and objectives. It should be user-friendly: a tone which every staff member, funder, administrator, and stakeholder can identify with and accept. Staff members should be able to view it as a guiding philosophy that directs and supports every decision.

While it should be reviewed periodically, a good mission statement should not need continued modification. Only a poorly written or excessively detailed statement requires continual modification. Figure 7-2 contains a sample of a mission statement workform.

Some sample mission statements appear below.

Most mission statements implicitly incorporate a set of values, which may be included in the mission statement or set out explicitly as a separate statement. Values relate more to qualitative issues

---

The mission of the university library is to support the quality of teaching, research, and service missions of the University as a state-wide comprehensive university providing access to recorded knowledge through the acquisition, organization, preservation and interpretation of information appropriate to current and future needs of the staff, faculty, students and the immediate community served by the library.

The mission of the public library is to identify, acquire, organize, publicize, and disseminate those resources which encourage and support through access to cultural and recreational resources and materials: life-long learning of our citizens; community, business and personal economic development; and citizens' personal growth and quality of life.

The mission of the corporate library is to provide the business and technical information required by corporate employees to meet successfully management's goals and objectives in a responsive, timely and cost-effective manner.

such as ethics and behavior than to the specific functions and services the library performs. Terms such as quality service, quality of life, respect for the individual and personal dignity are all examples of values. A formal, well-understood set of values creates an organizational climate that encourages and supports consistent treatment and behavior. It provides guidelines that enable staff to act independently, while knowing that they are adhering to the organization's mores.

GOALS

While a mission statement provides the overall guiding vision for the institution, the more detailed goals that define the broad strategies an institution will pursue in support of its mission provide further definition of this statement. Ideally these goals should be limited in number, preferably from five to eight. When a library tries to pursue too many goals, it can lose its focus and accomplish nothing. Each of the goals is then further amplified by a set of measurable objectives, which in turn are supported by action plans. Goals should describe a library's broad aims with respect to programs such as:

>Preservation
>Young adult or undergraduate services
>Outreach or branch services
>Collection development
>Network participation
>Other broadly focused programs

Statements of goals should be easy to understand and remember and should reflect qualitative as opposed to quantitative concerns. Examples of some goal statements are:

>To provide quality reference services to library users.
>To select, acquire, process and maintain those resources that best support library users.
>To use technology as appropriate to enhance the library's ability to serve its clientele.
>To communicate promptly and effectively with the library's clientele, staff, advisory groups and institutional management.

STRATEGIC FOCUS **65**

FIGURE 7-2 MISSION STATEMENT WORKFORM

```
Community served:



Broad services:



Library values:
```

Figure 7-3 is an example of a goals workform.

OBJECTIVES

In contrast to goals, objectives are short-term, specific and measurable. They include some unit and time specification. Objectives should address how the library will fulfill its mission. They should relate to one or more goals, and be realistic, achievable and understandable. Objectives require the library to commit resources. Some sample objectives are:

> Review, update and complete library collection development policy by June 199x.

FIGURE 7-3 GOALS WORKFORM

1.

2.

3.

4.

5.

Open new branch library in ———— by June 199x.

Questions to ask in developing a specific objective are:

Has a specific date for completion been identified?
Have specific results been identified?
Are these results measurable? (Will you know when you are done?)
Can others see the relationship between the objective and the goal it supports?

Figure 7-4 is an objectives workform.

ACTION PLANS

Action plans identify the specific steps and tasks needed to accomplish an objective. They include a task definition that answers the questions:

How will the task be done with clearly defined milestones for measuring completion?
Who will do the task?
What resources will be required?
When it will start?
How long it will take?
When it will be finished?
Is the beginning or completion of the task dependent on the completion of another task?

Figures 7-5 and 7-6 are examples of specific library action plans and Figure 7-7 shows an action plan workform.

Although in a very small library this hierarchical structure is unnecessary, in most institutions the amount of detail contained in the action plans is needed by staff to implement the plans.

When communicating the plan outside the library, some libraries will communicate only the mission and goals, while others will include objectives. Few will communicate all detailed action plans outside the library, although they may do so selectively. Content and communication are discussed more fully in Chapter 9.

FIGURE 7-4 OBJECTIVES WORKFORM

GOAL:

OBJECTIVES:

1.

2.

3.

4.

5.

6.

FIGURE 7-5 REBECCA CROWN LIBRARY, ROSARY COLLEGE, ACTION PLAN EXTRACT

GOAL: Assess the strength of academic support programs

SUBGOAL: Provide library services commensurate with needs of academic community

STRATEGY: Expand collection in weak areas subject to regular review RCPD Reference II,C,1,a,b,c

RESPONSIBLE OFFICE (DEPT. OR UNIT): Director of Library

CHAIR

ANALYSIS OF GOAL:

ACTION STEPS	TIMING Start Finish	RESOURCES REQUIRED (Human, financial, physical...)	BY WHOM
1. Maintain and expand holdings, including periodicals, especially in Business, Computer Science and Special Education	1986 on-going	Place orders for 70 new periodical titles mostly in areas of business, computer science and special-education. Review and continued support-incremental increases in subscription budget	Librarians in cooperation with faculty
2. Regularly review Government Documents Collection to keep it useful and current Create new shelflist	Annual and Continuous Jan 1987 Dec 1987	1/3 professional staff/15 hours per week student Does not require substantial financial resources	Serials librarian
3. Review and, if necessary, increase departmental book funding to better meet student needs			

FURTHER COMMENTS:

Reprinted with the permission of the Rebecca Crown Library, Rosary College

FIGURE 7-6 UMPQUA COMMUNITY COLLEGE LIBRARY LONG-RANGE PLAN EXTRACT

Goals	Measurable Objectives	Tasks & Events	Resources Required	Cost	Timeframe
Increase faculty use of professional library	* 10% circulation increase by June 1986	* List of items in professional library	Work-study	Minimal	June 1985
		* Open house	Staff	Minimal	January 1985, January 1986
		* New acquisition list, items separate by collection; copies for person rather than building	Staff and work-study	Supplies, $30.00	Begin April 1985
		* Keep records of professional library circulation	Staff		Begin summer 1985
		* Provide job opportunity listing in looseleaf	Cooperation of personnel department	0	April 1985
Improve library	* Increase student library use 8% by June 1986	* Term paper clinics	Staff cooperation of student newspaper, other publicity	0	Begin fall 1985
	* Improve library literacy 20% by June 1988; 10% per year thereafter	* Class library projects. Test of library literacy	Faculty	$20,000 for full-time librarians	Begin spring 1985
		* Class in library use			Fall or summer 1985
		* Dialog demos online	Budget	Begin $1,500/year	1986
		* Magazine index	Budget	$1,300/year	1986
Strength staff	* Full-time clerk-typist to to replace one half-time		Budget		Summer 1985
	* Full-time librarians to replace half-time (reference, instruction, assist director)			See above	Summer 1986

Reprinted with permission from Umpqua Community College Library (Roseburg, OR)

FIGURE 7-7 ACTION PLANS WORKFORM

GOAL:

OBJECTIVE:

Action	Resources needed	Who	Start Date	Completion Date	Goals Supporte

STRATEGIC FOCUS

POLICIES AND PROCEDURES

Once the library has completed the statement of its mission, goals and objectives, it should review both institutional and library policies and procedures. Where institutional policies are incompatible with those needed by the library, the library should investigate with the appropriate institutional officers how firm these are and whether these policies and procedures can be changed. If it is not possible to change these policies and procedures in the short term, consider whether their impact on the plan will necessitate any changes. In the long term, change in institutional policies is possible provided that managers are willing to make the necessary efforts. They should focus on the issues that really matter and not waste time and energy on issues that make no real difference.

Library policies and procedures should be compatible with and support strategic planning objectives. If they do not, they should be revised. Policies related to performance and review are particularly important. Performance review and rewards should be an integral part of the process of achieving strategic objectives and completing action plan milestones. Those libraries having civil service regulations, faculty tenure systems or unions may face challenges in these areas, but over time even these regulations and agreements can, with work and sufficient political savvy, be aligned with strategic planning requirements. In the interim, some adjustments to the plan may be necessary, but they should be made with the library's mission and long-term objectives in mind.

Policy revisions will obviously depend on which policies are affected and whether they relate to a single unit or to the library as a whole. A written procedure related to developing, revising or withdrawing policies and procedures should be in place. If not, one should be developed. Ideally the manager of the affected area should develop the necessary formal statement in consultation with staff, and have it approved by senior management and institutional groups as needed. Senior management could delegate the task of library-wide policy review and development to one of the senior management team or a task force. Since the policies and procedures identified as needing revision or development directly relate to the strategic plan, the core planning team may assume the responsibility for initiating revision subject to senior management approval. It is essential that the policy and procedure revisions are consistent with and support the library's chosen mission and goals.

SUMMARY

The heart of the plan and its driving force, the library's mission statement is amplified by broad goals, reinforced by measurable objectives and fundamentally supported by detailed action plans that include a schedule, milestones, deliverable results and a list of responsible individuals and units. The mission and goals broadly describe what a library does and for whom. The objectives specifically describe when and how the library will accomplish its mission. The action plans identify the specific tasks needed to complete an objective; they answer the questions: who, what, where, when and how the objectives are to be completed. Together these elements constitute most of the strategic plan and define the strategic focus. Priority setting and resources allocation are considered next.

8 VALUES, PRIORITIES, AND RESOURCES

Values
Value-added Services
   VAT
   Factors
   Taylor's Model
   Government Data Bases
Priorities
   Models
Resource Allocation
Summary

Among the most difficult challenges affecting a library or information center manager are the establishment of suitable values and priorities and the allocation of the necessary resources. In exploring this process, the manager must consider several concepts or processes, including value and value-added services, planning and goal setting and resource allocation.

VALUES

Value-added services has become a fashionable phrase. Libraries are increasingly being asked what value they provide to justify their budgets and even their very existence. In many places, it is no longer accepted that libraries will be supported because they are inherently good. Consequently, librarians and information center managers must have a thorough understanding of values and their impact on their libraries and information centers.

Values and value perceptions differ among librarians, institutional administrators, and boards and groups and classes of users. The great diversity in values arises from varying experiences, personal values, societal values, and a complex array of other variables, as shown in Figure 8-1. An individual's value system determines the value the person places on goods, services, products and relationships and the individual's perception of those items. James Anderson in *Public Policy-Making*,[1] Robert S. Taylor in *Value-Added Processes in Information Systems*[2] and Bruce P. Schauer in *The Economics of Managing Library Service*[3] explore certain aspects of this subjectivity, although Schauer talks in the economists' terms of utility and restricts his discussion accordingly. Readers interested a discussion from an economist's point of view on utility should refer to Schauer.

In his work, Taylor discusses many aspects of the subjective nature of value, as does Jacob in an article for *The Bottom Line*.[4] Rather than providing a single definition of values, Taylor instead provides a series depending on the context. This manual, however, will use Jacob's simple dictionary definition: "the worth of property, goods, services."[5] Since the discussion in Taylor is far more extensive, those who read it will find it informative.

An administrator must understand that value depends on the perceptions of the people from whom she is asking support. While it is important to recognize the values of the library's clientele since they are the ultimate arbiters of a whether a library is fulfilling its

76 STRATEGIC PLANNING

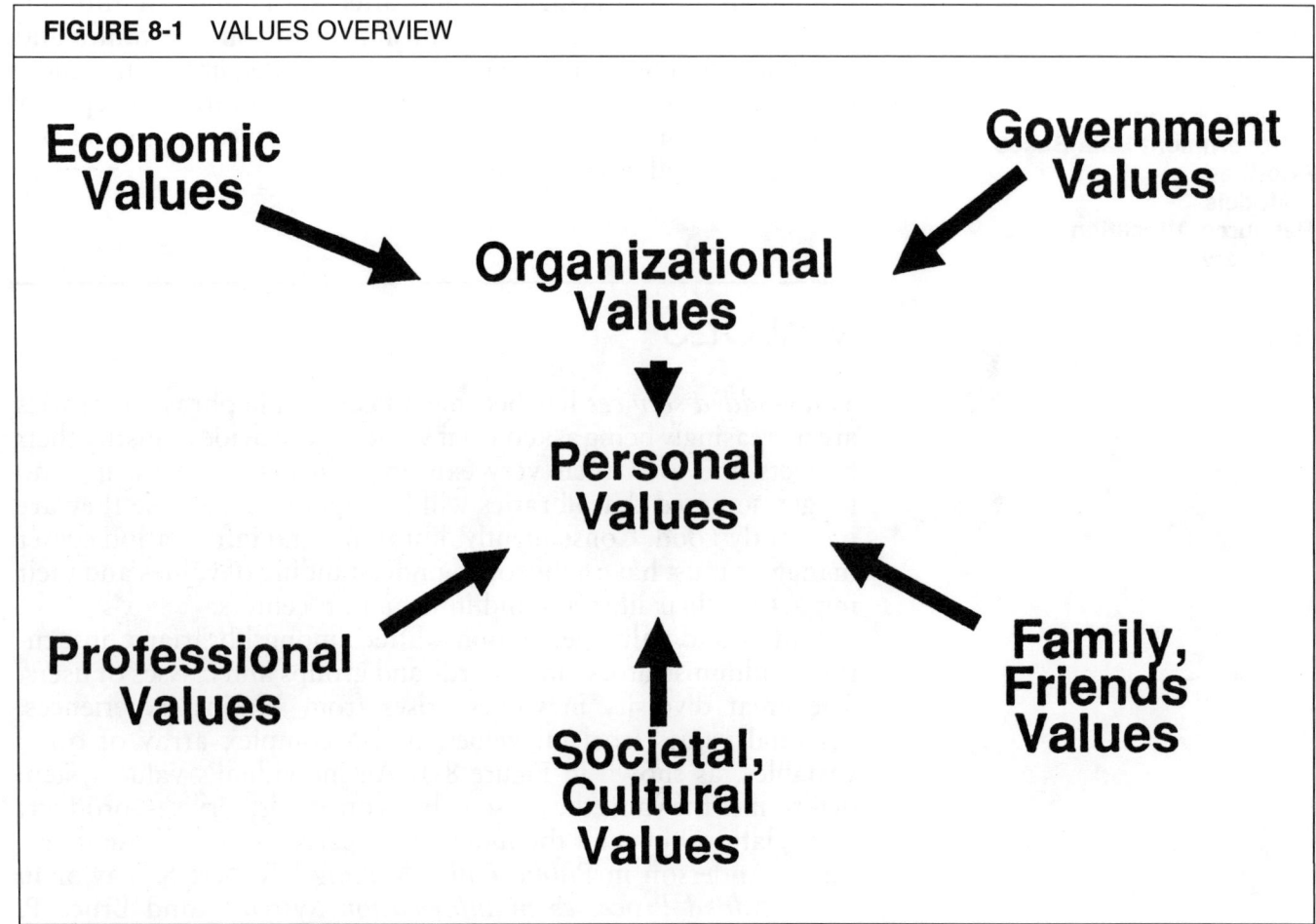

FIGURE 8-1 VALUES OVERVIEW

mission, they are not typically the funders. When public libraries seek bond issues or other publicly supported finance, the voters' perceptions are paramount.

However, since the funders in most instances are separate from the clientele, they may have an entirely different value system. Public, academic and corporate administrators all exhibit concerns over cost control and effective use of resources. Boards usually have a fiduciary responsibility that requires them to ensure that library resources are effectively used. Boards are typically more interested in modestly increasing the budget to keep pace with inflation, maintaining a static budget, or reducing budgets in times of institutional pressure rather than being interested in increasing services. In addition to managing the cost base of the library, effective resource allocation and augmentation of institutional resources, the library manager must understand the value systems of these groups, and determine how to use concepts and tools such as value-added and modeling to appeal to such groups.

VALUE-ADDED SERVICES

Some aspects of traditional economics and cost accounting theory are useful in understanding value-added concepts. Manufacturing processes start with raw materials which are then transformed by labor, machines, and processing into finished goods or products. The manufacturer then stores and eventually distributes these products to wholesalers, who in turn distribute them to retailers who sell the products to the ultimate consumers. As illustrated in Figure 8-2, each intermediate process adds some incremental value to the raw material as it is transformed into a manufactured product. These intermediate processes are the basis for European VAT (value-added tax), which is levied on a product as it moves from a manufacturer to a wholesaler to a retailer to the consumer. Each one pays a value-added tax on that portion of value added in the preceding process.

The value addition model can also apply by analogy to information products and services. Unlike manufactured products, information is not destroyed or worn out by consumption. The value of information to the user, however, may change; its value may be affected by its timeliness, location, ease of access, cost, form or use restrictions. Some information ages quickly and is of interest for only a limited time, while other information may increase in value as it ages. For example, weather information is most desirable before the forecasted weather occurs. It does, however, retain some value for those people who monitor long-term weather patterns. Lately, with the concern about global warming, past weather data has been heavily analyzed, and the conclusions of whether the world's weather is warming or merely erratic are hotly debated. For most people, yesterday's weather is of no interest. Once known, information may increase or decrease in value as it is applied. For instance, its value to others may be greater than to the original user.

Having already acquired information, a user will not pay again to acquire the same data unless it is packaged in a form that is easier to use or is inseparable from other desired information. The cost of information may also affect its value to the user. If the cost to

FIGURE 8-2 VALUE-ADDED MANUFACTURING

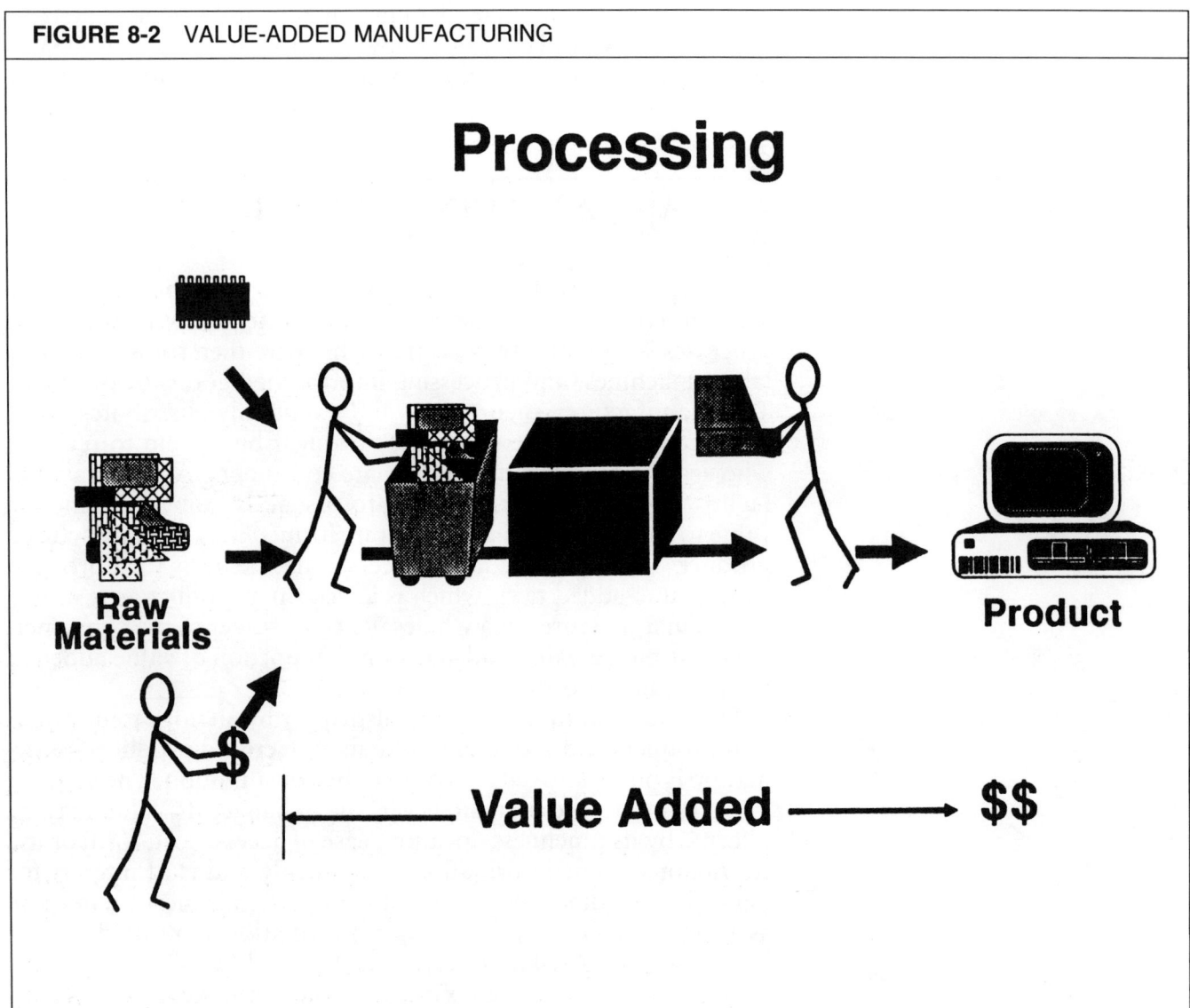

acquire the information is greater than the loss or risk of not having it, the user may decide that the information is not sufficiently valuable to buy. The user may buy the information at one price, but not at a higher price. A book on strategic planning at $35 is more likely to be purchased than one at $100.

Restrictions on the ability to copy, reuse or transmit information to others may diminish its usefulness and, consequently, its value. For some users, restricted access to information may enhance its value. If they can acquire it, but their competitor cannot, the restriction may provide an advantage. Exclusive licensing and contractual agreements for celebrity endorsements are examples of restrictions that enhance value. Pepsi and Coca-Cola are paying exorbitant fees to celebrities to advertise their products. Pop singer Madonna reportedly signed a $10,000,000 contract with Pepsi for commercials. (Ironically, adverse publicity associated with a Madonna video has caused Pepsi to reconsider plans to feature the singer.)

Most recently, a furor has arisen over the proposed Library of Congress licensing agreement for LC MARC tapes. Hard pressed financially and concerned over the integrity and repackaging of LC MARC records, LC sought through licensing agreements to retain more control over the use of LC records. The proposed licensing agreement prompted an outcry by vendors and librarians who faced higher costs and greater restrictions.

LC has announced its intention to restudy the issue and has decided not to proceed with licensing at this time. The revisions to the Paperwork Reduction Act, HR 2381 may influence the final result. The Act contains specific provisions regarding the distribution of and the costs for government information. Ironically, the proposed licensing comes at a time when LC is increasing its distribution of records contributed to LC by other libraries and some vendors.

Taylor's model of the information process is illustrated in Figure 8-3. It treats data as the raw material. The data is transformed into action in several discrete stages. Moreover, it should be noted that the transformation of information into action is not always immediate. Some information is sought to satisfy a current problem, but other information that does not have an immediate application may lie dormant until a problem or context arises to which it can be applied.

Taylor's model of the information process and his ensuing discussion are particularly interesting because he focuses on the process of transforming data into information and finally into action. As shown in Figure 8-4, publishers add value to information by selecting material to publish; editing and enhancing the material; packaging it into books and journals; and warehousing, distributing, advertising, and selling the finished products to libraries, bookstores and readers. As shown in Figure 8-5, libraries add value by selecting materials; cataloging and storing them; enhancing access to them; retrieving them; lending them; recording and tracking use of them; and maintaining them, to list a few aspects of library service.

Each time information is processed to improve access to it, to

80 STRATEGIC PLANNING

FIGURE 8-3 ROBERT TAYLOR'S MODEL OF VALUE-ADDED INFORMATION SERVICES

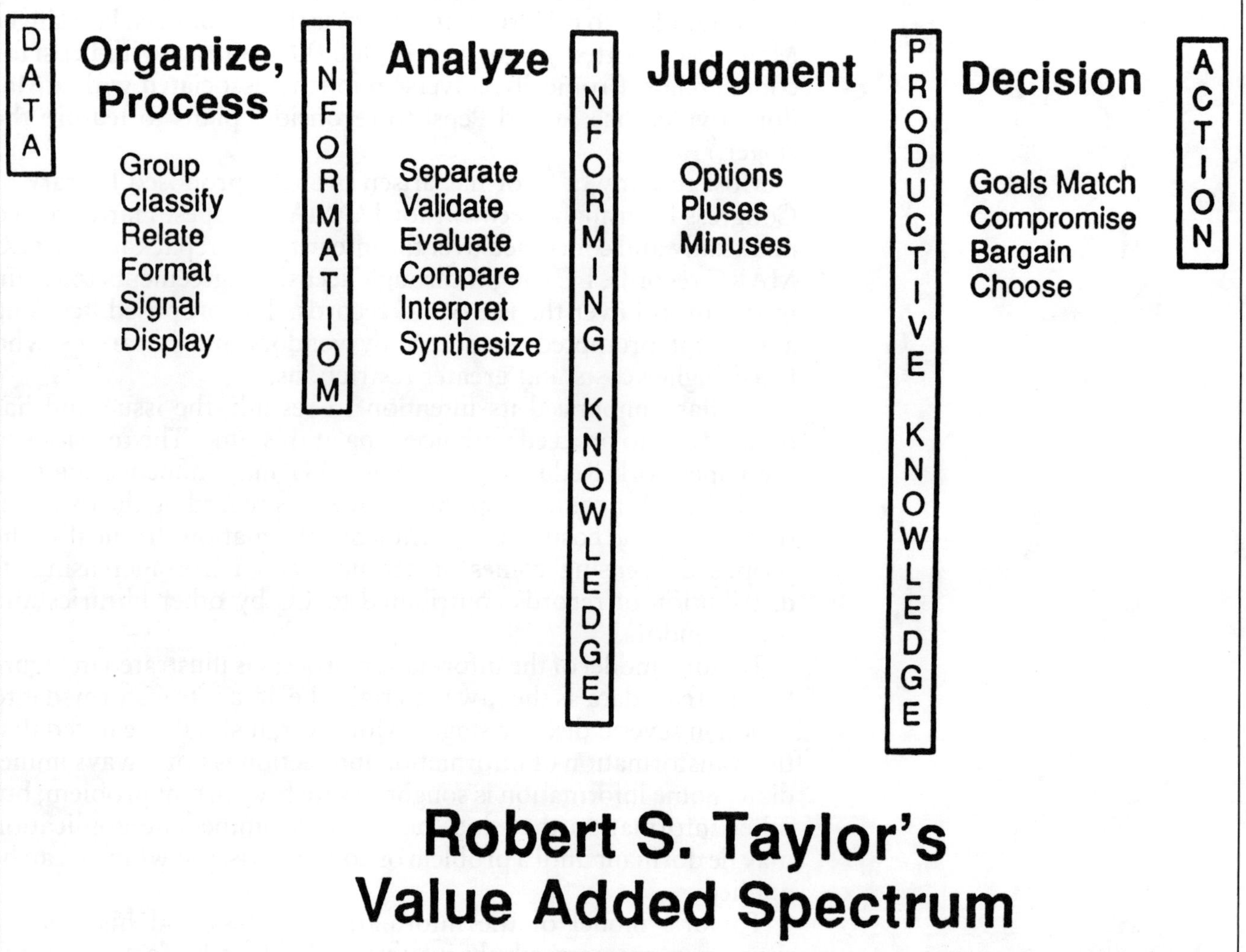

DATA | **Organize, Process** | INFORMATION | **Analyze** | INFORMING KNOWLEDGE | **Judgment** | PRODUCTIVE KNOWLEDGE | **Decision** | ACTION

Organize, Process:
- Group
- Classify
- Relate
- Format
- Signal
- Display

Analyze:
- Separate
- Validate
- Evaluate
- Compare
- Interpret
- Synthesize

Judgment:
- Options
- Pluses
- Minuses

Decision:
- Goals Match
- Compromise
- Bargain
- Choose

Robert S. Taylor's Value Added Spectrum

Adapted from Robert S. Taylor, <u>Value-Added Processes in Information Systems</u>.

enhance its usability in format or content, to bring it to a new audience, to relate it to other information, to lower its cost or to change it in some way that the user perceives as important, the value of that information increases. In the United States, federal government information, depending on the type and distribution restrictions, can be purchased from the U.S. Government Printing

Office, the National Technical Information Service, directly from individual government agencies or from a number of commercial firms. The commercial firms may repackage and/or enhance access to government information. For example, OCLC repackages the ERIC and Agricola data bases and combines them with OCLC bibliographic records to provide a more comprehensive tool for reference use. A number of libraries provide enhanced access to

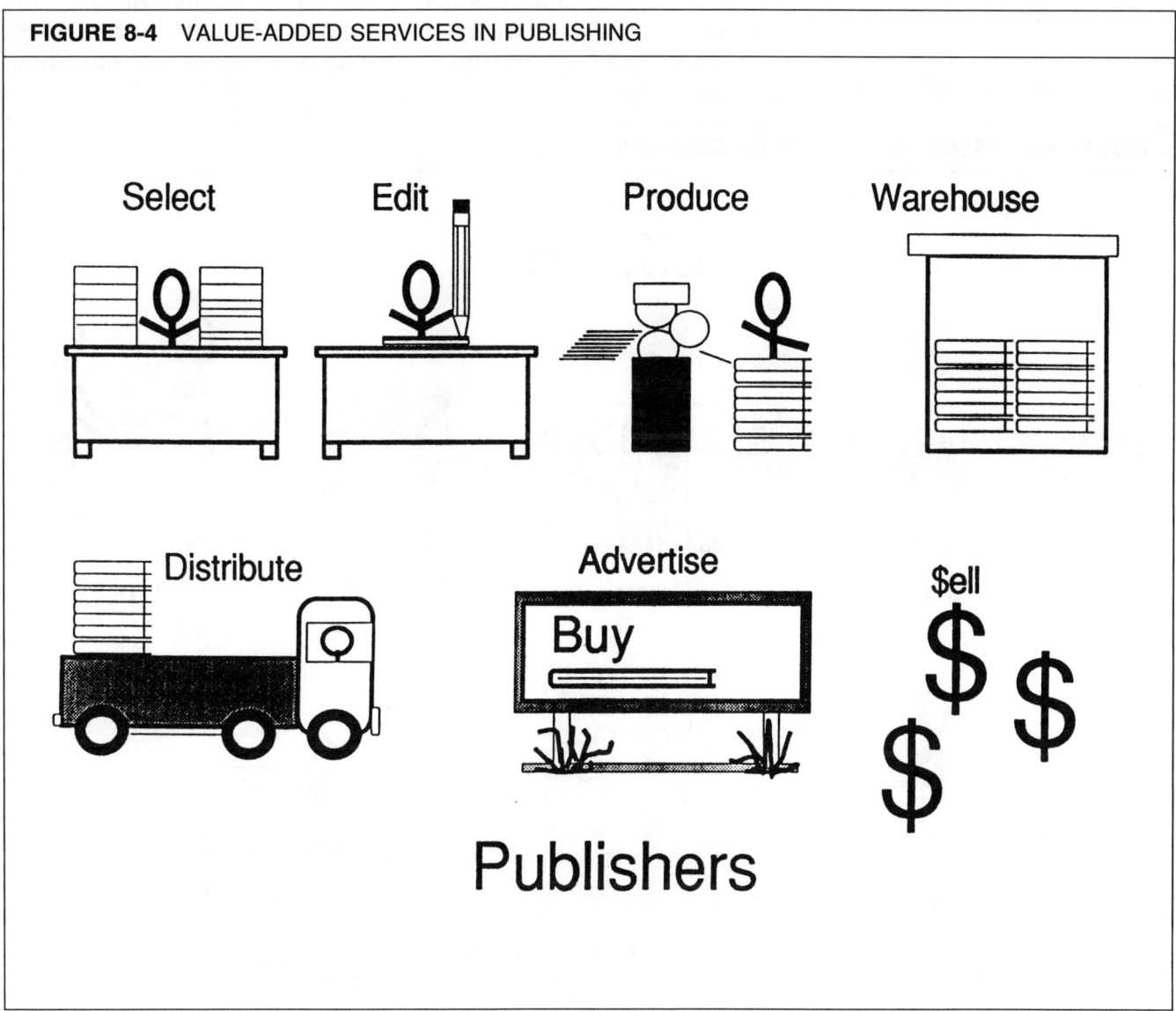

FIGURE 8-4 VALUE-ADDED SERVICES IN PUBLISHING

82 STRATEGIC PLANNING

local materials by creating and publishing special indexes such as for local newspapers or for photograph collections.

PRIORITIES

A library cannot set priorities without a clear vision of both its role and the user community's perceptions of the relative values of the various actions and functions required to attain that vision. More libraries are using strategic planning as a means of establishing

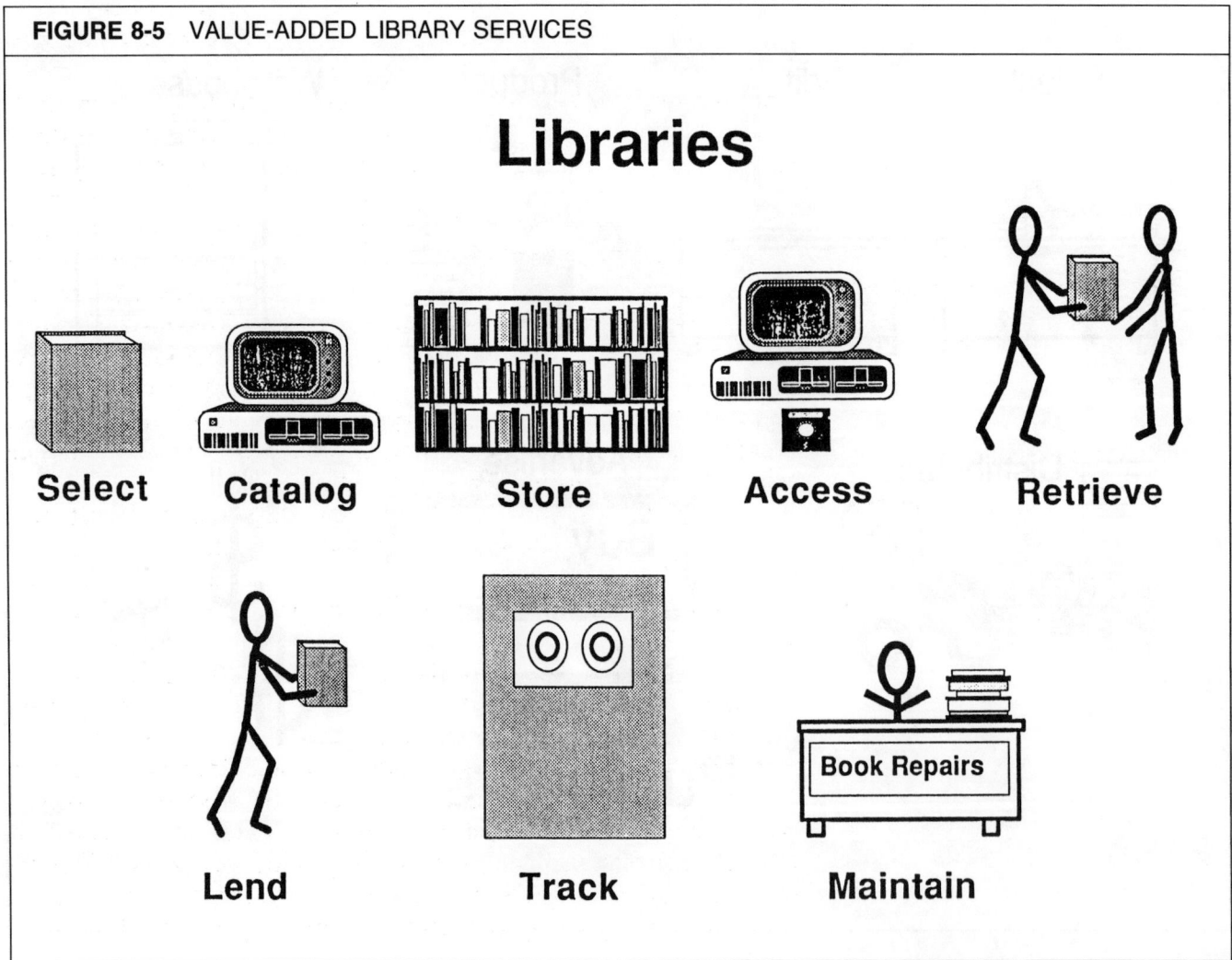

FIGURE 8-5 VALUE-ADDED LIBRARY SERVICES

such a vision and setting priorities. A 1987 survey encompassing some 3,000 institutions within the OCLC community of libraries indicated that 33 percent have planning processes which they use.[6] Some use the planning process to maintain present resources or acquire new resources. To cope with economic constraints, others use planning as a means of managing with reduced resources.

Models

A model developed by Jacob in 1982 provides a means to consider and assess the various alternatives for allocating resources.[7] The concept behind the model was to look at a library's budget from two perspectives: a goal- and activity-driven model and a resource-driven model. Figure 8-6 shows the two perspectives. Many library directors use rule-of-thumb measures. For example, a manager might calculate that x new books require y catalogers or adding a new service will require z staff to cover the hours of service. Jacob's model is a more formal way of relating such variables to each other. Using a specified set of activity levels following certain parameters for library productivity (i.e. number of books processed or the number of circulation transactions), a manager can calculate the budget level and staff resources needed. Alternatively, the manager can feed prescribed resource parameters into the spreadsheet model which will provide the activity levels that can be supported. From either perspective, the manager can vary the parameters and can assess the impact of these changes on services, activity levels, staffing and funding. The manager can select the most appropriate combination.

This particular model was translated into a spreadsheet program for computer manipulation. Similar models can be found in Clark[8] and Machalow.[9] The Los Angeles County Public Library and the University of California library system have made extensive use of such models.

A model does not make decisions. It merely allows the manager to assess better the potential impact of decisions and to alter priorities as needed. The manager can look at the effects of different choices on staffing, resources or activity levels and then choose the combination that produces the best set of results within the constraints imposed by budget or staffing levels. Alternatively, the manager can justify adding resources or staff. Whether computer- or paper-based, models are another tool to assist decision making; however, they are not a substitute for astute judgment.

84 STRATEGIC PLANNING

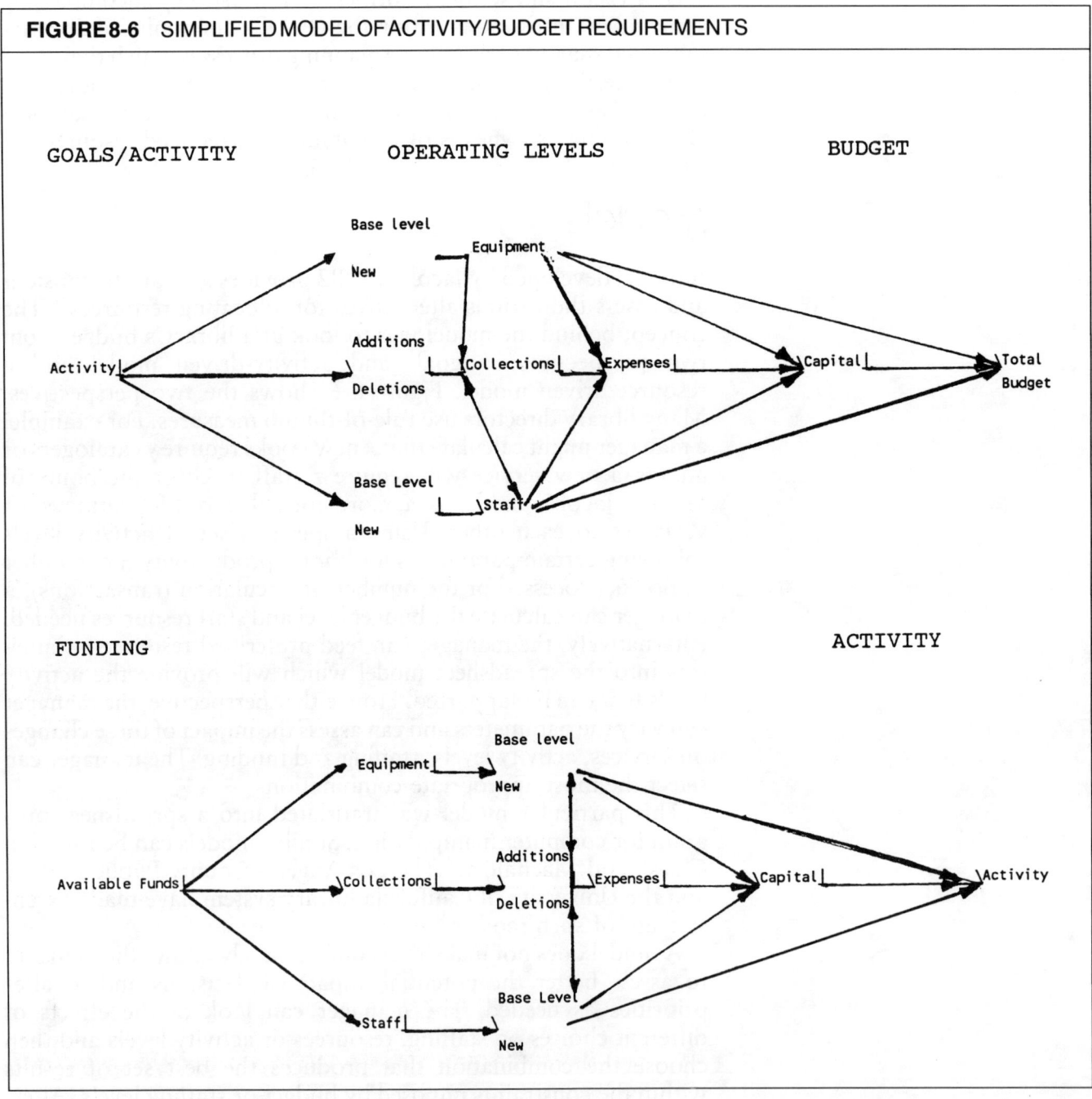

FIGURE 8-6 SIMPLIFIED MODEL OF ACTIVITY/BUDGET REQUIREMENTS

Models make some important assumptions, which vary with the particular model and its parameters. Typical assumptions might include:

The productivity rate of various library staff
The amount of materials to be acquired
The complexity of the work involved
Peak work loads

The degree to which assumptions are realistic will affect the success of the model in representing library functions, in usefully assessing alternatives and in helping to evaluate various priorities.

RESOURCE ALLOCATION

When setting priorities and allocating resources, a manager must consider the value systems of those to whom the library is responsible, including funders, administrators and clientele. These values should be among the values upon which the library's mission and goals have been built. If the plan has been responsive to the library's clientele, it will provide a strong tool for identifying and later acquiring the necessary resources.

Much of a manager's effectiveness in resource allocation depends on the ability to secure commitment to goals and to gain access to resources to support those goals. Resources are not limited solely to those provided by the parent institution or primary funding source. Increasing numbers of libraries are hiring development officers to help locate and acquire other sources of funds. These sources include:

Community fund raising programs
Foundation support
Donor programs
Corporate contributors
Regional, state, or federal agency funds
Endowment programs
Traditional bake and book sales

The point is that resources are limited only if a manager believes they are. By exercising creativity and ingenuity, a library can tap new sources of revenue.

Whatever the cycle for the institution or library budget is, budget requests should be driven by the library plan and its overall resources. Once the library's funding source has accepted a planning document, budget requests should always refer back to the strategic plan and to the particular goals and objectives the requested resources are needed to support. If for any reason, budget requests are refused, the library should consider whether alternate funding is possible and seek it. If funds cannot be found, the manager should consider the impact on the plan and its implementation. Contingency plans should be available from some of the scenario work discussed in Chapter 6.

SUMMARY

To manage a library successfully, a manager must know and work with the value system of the community served, must develop an acceptable set of goals and a realistic means of achieving those goals, must acquire or allocate the necessary resources to achieve those goals and finally must monitor progress on achieving those goals and adjust the plans and resources as needed. Setting priorities is an iterative process that must be continually refined. Librarians are increasingly using technology and tools along with professional expertise and judgment to better manage libraries.

REFERENCES

1. James E. Anderson, *Public Policy-Making*, 3rd ed. (New York: Holt Rinehart Winston, 198?). 0-03-062394-4.
2. Robert S. Taylor, *Value-Added Processes in Information Systems*. (Norwood, New Jersey: Ablex, 1986). 0-89391-273-5. LCCN 85-18677
3. Bruce P. Schauer, *The Economics of Managing Library Service*. (Chicago: A.L.A., 1986). 0-8389-0453-X. LCCN 86-14186.
4. M.E.L. Jacob, "Costing and Pricing: the Difference Matters," *Bottom Line* 2(2) (1988):12-14.
5. M.E.L. Jacob, *Planning in OCLC Member Libraries*, ed. asst. Sondra Albanese, *OCLC Library, Information, and Computer Science Series*, 9, (Dublin, Ohio: OCLC, 1988). 1-55653-051-X.
6. Ibid.
7. M.E.L. Jacob, "Online Economics: the Network Perspective," Proceedings of Fourth National Online Meeting. (Medford, New Jersey: Learned Information, 1983) 253-4 (abstract only).
8. Philip Clark, *Microcomputer Spreadsheet Models for Libraries*. (Chicago: A.L.A., 1985).

9. Robert Machalow, *Using Lotus 1-2-3: A How-to-do-it Manual for Library Applications,* (New York: Neal-Schuman, 1989).

9 PLAN FORMAT AND COMMUNICATION

Audience and Message
How to Communicate
When to Communicate
Resources
Summary

The manager and planner have spent considerable effort and time in gathering and analyzing information, used that information to develop a vision and mission, formulated goals and objectives to support that mission, prioritized those goals and objectives, developed action plans and schedules and developed resource allocation plans to support all of these. The next major step, and the first step in the implementation process, is communication of the plan. The communication plan involves specifying the content and format of the strategic plan, identifying the audience and determining how and when to communicate the plan to its targeted audience.

To communicate effectively, certain principles are useful. By answering the following questions, a manager or planner can identify the plan information that should be communicated:

Who is the primary audience?
What is the primary message?
How the message can best be communicated?
When should the message be communicated?
What resources are necessary for the communication piece?

Figure 9-1 contains a communications checklist.

AUDIENCE AND MESSAGE

Plans can be expressed in various physical forms. The manager must select and design the plan content and format to relate to the plan's target audience. Depending on the type of library, the target audience may be:

Parent institution administrators
Library advisory groups
Boards of trustees
Library management and staff
Library clientele
Communities served

Time is valuable to parent organization administrators, most of whom prefer not to wade through hundreds of pages of unnecessary detail. Ideally, they want to learn quickly the focus of the plan, the resources necessary to accomplish the plan, and the benefits the library and the parent organization will receive in exchange for

FIGURE 9-1 COMMUNICATIONS PLAN CHECKLIST

1. Who is the target/primary audience?
   - Library staff
   - Parent institution administrators
   - Board or advisory group
   - Users
   - Potential users
   - Funding agency or foundation
   - Business community

2. What is the message?
   - Announcement of start of planning
   - Communication about plan or plan progress
   - Assumptions, environmental scan
   - Summary of the plan
   - Contents of the plan (see Figure 9-2)
   - Request for resources or support

3. What communication media and format will be used?
   - Newsletter or newspaper article
   - Brochure
   - Meeting
   - Radio or television spot, interview or announcement
   - Flyers, bookmarks, t-shirts, cups, bags or other publicity devices

4. What is the communication schedule?
   - Monthly reports on progress
   - News of the completion of significant milestones
   - Annual updates on environment, assumptions and goals
   - Complete revision of the plan every three to five years

5. What resources are required?
   - Compilation and analysis of data for communication piece
   - Staff time
   - Word processing or graphical design work
   - Reproduction and distribution costs (and postage)
   - Professional or consultant fees

PLAN FORMAT AND COMMUNICATION   91

Communication of the Plan

Step 1
Identify the audience

Step 2
Identify the message

Step 3
Adapt the message to specific audiences
—Executive summary for parent organization administrators, boards and advisory committees
—Detailed action plan for planning team, management and staff

providing those resources. For this audience, a tightly summarized version of the plan is essential.

The summary should contain the mission statement, a description of its relationship to the parent institution's mission, the main goals and objectives, and a broad plan showing a schedule and the projected resources needed. The summary is also useful in working with boards and advisory committees. The communications checklist in Figure 9-1 provides questions that are helpful in planning the summary, while the executive summary section in Figure 9-2 defines the essential content. Managers and planners should ensure that the summary contains the major results to be achieved, in concrete, measurable form, and the associated resources required to achieve them.

More detailed action plans are essential for the operational management, implementation, and monitoring of plan progress. While senior library management may review and approve action plans, the operating units will use the action plans to identify tasks and establish work unit goals.

Figure 9-2 provides an outline of what the library strategic plan should contain. The plan should be a concise document that contains conclusions and supporting data presented in graphic and chart form. The main text should only contain:

    A strategic focus consisting of:
        Mission
        Goals
        Objectives
        Priorities

    An operating plan consisting of:
        Action plan with schedules and results
        Resources

Certain supporting materials may appear in the appendices, but not in the main text. Such items include:

    Plan rationale
    Assumptions
    Key environmental trends
    Parent institution mission, goals and objectives (highlighting those related to the library)
    Summary of the library's assessment (strengths, weaknesses, clientele needs, threats and unexploited opportunities)
    Scenarios

FIGURE 9-2 STRATEGIC PLAN OUTLINE

```
                                                      Chapter  Status

  1.   Executive Summary                                 9       D
       (highlights only)
       Mission
       Goals
       Objectives
       Resources

  2.   Strategic Focus                                   7,9     E
       Mission/Values                                    7       E
       Goals                                             7       E
       Objectives                                        7       E

  3.   Operating Plan                                    7,8     E
       Priorities                                        8       E
       Action Plans                                      7       R
       Resources                                         8       E

Appendices
Rationale                                                3       R
Assumptions                                              5       E
Key environmental trends                                 6       E
Parent mission/goals/objectives (or assumed goals)       4       R
Summary of library assessment                            6       R
Scenarios                                                6       R
Planning process                                         3       R
     Model used                                          3       R
     Key players/roles                                   3       R
     Cycle for creating, monitoring, updating            9       R
     Documents, reports produced                         3       R
Alignment of policies and procedures                     7       R

D = Desirable      E = Essential     R = Recommended
```

Planning process
Alignment of policies and procedures

Both the plan and its supporting materials should appear in highly summarized format using graphics and charts. Explanatory text should appear only when necessary. Persons looking at the plan should be able to grasp the key points quickly.

The primary purpose of the full written plan is to document the plan and to communicate it succinctly and unambiguously to others. This is not the place for long, extended explanations. The plan should not resemble a technical report, literary essay, journal article, or political tract.

Planning staff or designated managers should update the plan at least annually, and the new version should clearly indicate what progress has been made. For example, highlighting segments of timelines or specific milestones could illustrate what has been completed and what changes have been needed. If the document is brief and focused and contains limited text, this task will be easier. Project management software can reduce the time and effort required to update and reproduce action plans and associated schedules with timelines and milestones.

One version of plans that has been used successfully by several organizations is a highly summarized statement designed to communicate with staff, users, and other stakeholders. Such plans may appear in brochure form or even in the form of a short report. Examples in Figures 9-3 through 9-5 include AT&T Bell Laboratories Library and Information Systems Center, OCLC and Las Vegas-Clark County Library District.

The planner or manager must remember what audience they are communicating with and what information they want to communicate to that audience. Language, style, physical layout, and the liberal use of graphics are critical elements in successfully conveying a message. The dictum of public speaking also applies to strategic planning: "Tell them what you plan to tell them, tell them, and then tell them what you told them." Graphics can reinforce the message; readers generally understand graphs and bar charts more easily than tables of numbers. With the tools available on most personal computers, there is no excuse for not producing high-quality, low-cost graphics. Creativity in presentation and communication is just as important as creativity in planning.

HOW TO COMMUNICATE

While written forms of the plan can be effective communication tools, managers and planners should supplement them with meet-

FIGURE 9-3 AT&T BELL LIBRARIES MISSION STATEMENT

Human Resource Commitment

Libraries and Information Systems Center

It is essential that all staff understand their responsibilities and how they can contribute in pursuing these service commitments. Management must assure that each individual recognizes the importance of her/his role in this effort. Further, management recognizes that the Center's success depends on each individual's success and is committed to establishing a work environment in which each individual can achieve her/his work objectives effectively and efficiently in an innovative and timely manner.

W David Penniman
Director, Libraries and
Information Systems Center
AT&T Bell Laboratories

AT&T

4/86

MISSION

To provide technical, business and marketplace information services needed by individuals & groups within AT&T at competitive cost.

The Center is in the business of:

- designing, developing & managing technical, business & marketplace information systems and services

- providing a resource-sharing network that links the information services of dispersed sites within AT&T

- managing internally generated AT&T technical information and assuring its full and proper use.

Service Commitments

To carry out these enterprises we will:

- Monitor the changing interests of individuals & organizations served by the Library Network, operated by AT&T Bell Laboratories, to anticipate and satisfy their information needs.

- Identify and promptly make available relevant internally - and externally - generated information in all disciplines & formats required to support the needs of users.

- Facilitate the use of information through the development and provision of specialized, value-added information services such as alerting bulletins, foreign language services, online literature searching, marketplace monitoring or subject-oriented specialized activities.

- Manage the distribution of AT&T proprietary information to assure that it is available to those within AT&T who have need of it, and to assure that proprietary information is protected.

- Make information readily accessible by designing & managing libraries, access stations & other specialized information-handling systems.

- Apply the latest appropriate information handling technologies and processes to assure that services are delivered in a cost effective manner.

FIGURE 9-4 OCLC STRATEGIC PLANNING BROCHURE

- Exploit the capabilities of the micro- or personal computer in the context of the OCLC Online System, local systems, and other local options.
- Continue, and expand as appropriate, national programs in cooperation with national agencies and associations.
- Implement strategies for expanded reference services and electronic information and document delivery.
- Expand in stages our new enhanced open telecommunications system that will cost-effectively support our online system as well as other new OCLC product/service offerings.
- Identify and respond to the special needs of and strengthen relationships with different types, sizes, and groups of libraries, institutions, and users.
- Enhance marketing and support services and strengthen OCLC/network relationships.
- Implement strategies to encourage international information exchange and improved access to worldwide information sources.

OCLC Online Computer Library Center, Inc., is a not-for-profit computer library service and research organization located in Dublin, Ohio, which provides centralized and local turnkey systems to libraries. The Center operates an international computer network that libraries use to acquire and catalog library materials, order custom-printed catalog cards, arrange interlibrary loans, and maintain location information on library materials. OCLC offers LS/2000, a local automated library system designed for an individual library or cluster of libraries.

Strategic Planning

We are engaged in the exciting and challenging process of developing a clear strategic vision of OCLC's future consistent with our broad public-purpose mission. To achieve this objective, in a constantly changing technological and economic environment, requires effective strategic planning. To me, it is not a governance function nor is it a particularly democratic function. It is a searching process that realistically assesses all kinds of contingencies and competitive developments in a disciplined way. It is also creative innovative predicting, sensing, brainstorming, and evaluating. We have made great strides, but it is a never-ending iterative process. Most of all, our strategic planning must focus on user needs in the broadest future context. Like all other critical activities at OCLC, it must be carried out with a bias toward commitment, action, and excellence.

Rowland C. W. Brown
President

Present and Future Functions

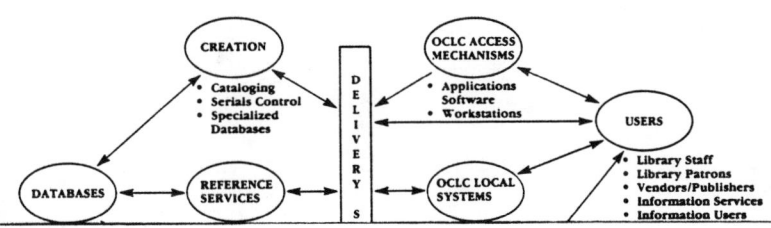

Corporate Charter

The purpose or purposes for which this Corporation is formed are to establish, maintain, and operate a computerized library network and to promote the evolution of library use, of libraries themselves, and of librarianship, and to provide processes and products for the benefit of library users and libraries, including such objectives as increasing availability of library resources to individual library patrons and reducing the rate-of-rise of library per unit costs, all for the fundamental public purpose of furthering ease of access to and use of the ever-expanding body of worldwide scientific, literary, and educational knowledge and information.

Situation Analysis
OCLC is an international bibliographic network serving all types of libraries. The corporation will provide new services consistent with its corporate charter.

Organizational Environment
- OCLC is a membership organization, a private corporation with public purposes. Its members elect Users Council delegates and board members.
- OCLC's services are made available primarily through state and regional networks.
- OCLC is a market-driven organization, responsive to user needs, but has constraints in terms of its
    Charter
    Governance
    Membership
    Not-for-profit status
- OCLC is moving to a new computer architecture and to an open telecommunications system.
- OCLC's rich and varied human resources include
    OCLC staff
    Networks
    Member libraries
    Vendors
- OCLC has a sound financial position.

Economic Environment
- Economic conditions have moderated, but libraries will continue to face increased competition for funding.
- OCLC has reached maturation of cataloging in academic libraries, but growth remains for other services.
- Growth potential exists in other segments, particularly in public and special libraries.
- Libraries and users are increasingly interested in electronic document delivery and enhanced services.
- The future is likely to be one of moderating economic conditions, with a moderate to high diffusion of technology.

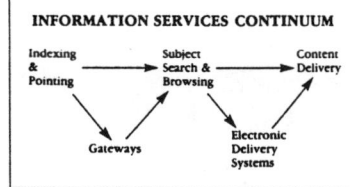

Implementation of Mission
To carry out its mission, OCLC will:

Continue to develop and maintain a strong *international* online bibliographic system serving a *broad range of types and sizes of libraries.*

- Preserve our present *de facto* national system as a national resource and extend, as appropriate, its international dimensions.
- Remain technically and economically viable.
- Add to the richness and integrity of the database to facilitate cataloging and resource sharing.
- Encourage responsible use of the system through education, pricing, copyright, contracts, and usage monitoring.
- Increase access to information in its myriad forms and facilitate its acquisition and use by libraries, library users, parent institutions and, where appropriate, by the general public.

Promote the evolution of library use, of libraries themselves, and librarianship; provide processes and products for the benefit of library users; and increase the availability of library resources to individual patrons through

- Research and development.
- Local-system and micro-based software enhancements.
- Reference services, databases, and gateways to other resources.
- Document delivery, electronic mail—information where, how, and when needed by users.
- Sensitivity to user needs for options and control balanced by responsible use.
- Strong training, support, and marketing function for online services, local systems, and other new products/services.
- Strong membership and user awareness of OCLC by libraries, information centers, and parent institutions.
- Development of public support.
- Staff and programs to serve identified needs of different types and sizes of libraries.

Maintain strong awareness of and support for OCLC and its public mission by

Networks
Libraries
Institutions
Library users
Government and government-sponsored entities
Foundations
Scholarly societies
Other library-related organizations

Maintain a leadership role in preparing libraries and institutions to fill their future roles through strong, broad research and development efforts.

- Conduct proprietary and nonproprietary research in support of library needs and OCLC's mission.
- Allocate a significant portion of OCLC's budget to research and development.
- Collaborate with others; support and/or purchase research; build on efforts of others to meet our objectives.
- Aggressively seek partnership or third-party funding

Corporate Strategic Directions
- Continue to maintain and improve the economic viability of the online system using available new technology.
- Offer new services as dictated by market needs, technology development, and OCLC capabilities.
- Expand local systems via LS/2000 and enhance mini- and micro-based offerings in the future and local system interfaces.

FIGURE 9-5 LAS VEGAS-CLARK COUNTY PUBLIC LIBRARY STRATEGIC PLAN BROCHURE

THE COMMITMENT TO THE FUTURE
A FIVE YEAR PLAN

MISSION STATEMENT

The mission of the Las Vegas-Clark County Library District is to serve the community as a resource center, providing every library patron with materials which satisfy the need for information, assist in the attainment of educational goals and promote the creative use of leisure time. The district's aim is to promote the value of information and to raise public awareness of those services which aid in the development of intellectual creativity and excellence.

THE CO...

The future in Southern N...
the past five years, 137,000 n...
the Las Vegas valley as their...
lation to 496,000 served by...
1988; and the trend contin...
future. In response, the Distri...
square feet to its present size...
next two years. Existing librari...
four new ones will be built i...
alone.

In addition to building ne...
trustees, the administration,...
determined to see that the...
Library District ranks nationa...
standing service, with emph...

GOAL 7

Investigate the most successful and creative library programs nationwide and adapt them to Las Vegas.

A. Accomplish at the end of two years a comprehensive review of innovative library programs from other communities with a promise of success in Las Vegas.

B. Within the two year period, implement one of the programs reviewed.

C. On an ongoing basis, review existing programs to insure that funds supporting them are justified.

The annual Art-A-Fair exhibit draws interested crowds.

GOAL 8

Develop private funding adequate for those functions and tasks which are desirable and which cannot be accomplished within the Library District's operating budget.

A. Bring the total funds raised privately to at least two per cent of the total annual library budget.

B. In each year of the plan, support with such funds the professional education of one children's librarian.

Seek adequate funding for public support of a new building program.

The Bucks for Books fundraiser is conducted annually.

ings and personal contact. Just as the manager or planner should create the written forms of the plan to reflect the intended audience, he or she should apply the same process and considerations to other types of communication. Ideally this has been defined within the planning process. The same audiences should be considered for these types of communication as for the written plan.

Normally, communicating with parent institution administrators is an ongoing process. Presumably, the manager has kept them fully informed during the development of the plan with periodic progress reports. In addition to submitting the written plan, the library director or planning team may also provide a more extensive briefing for this group, providing appropriate detail on priorities, results, and resources. By this point, the team should have clarified resource allocation needs. As a result of negotiations, either the parent has agreed to supply them or the library has made other plans for acquiring them.

One of the most crucial steps in implementing the plan consists of communicating with library management and staff. One communication technique that has worked for some organizations with staff is to meet with small groups (usually at the supervisory level) to brief them on the plan content, how to implement and monitor the plan and what roles they are expected to play. In a small library, the entire staff can be briefed. In a large organization, supervisors can take the responsibility for informing their individual staffs. Written documents appropriate to the group should reinforce the communication, such as library newsletter articles and reports, a brochure or leaflet on the plan or even sections of the plan related to their work. Most of this communication is part of the formalities associated with completing and implementing the plan. The planning team should have kept staff informed during the development of the plan both by using staff participation in task groups and by providing periodic reports. Such reports should continue during plan implementation. The success of the planning process and of the plan depends on good communication throughout the process, especially during the development, implementation and monitoring stages.

Similarly, open meetings held for library clientele and the communities served by the library would focus primarily on the mission, goals, objectives and tangible results that appeal to the particular group. Priorities would be a topic of particular interest. Depending on the resources plan, a discussion of how the library will acquire and use the necessary funding to achieve such results would also interest some groups. The format of the meetings should allow time for questions and a discussion. If members of these groups have been involved in formulating the plan, those persons can assist in communicating the plan to the community interests they represent.

WHEN TO COMMUNICATE

Once the plan has been completed, the management team should implement the communication process outlined above and should introduce the plan formally to those affected. Communication, however, ideally should begin with the start of the planning process and continue throughout the implementation cycle. Initial communiques will consist of press releases and articles in the library and institution newsletters. Some of the interim planning documents such as assumptions, key environmental trends, scenarios and draft mission statements should be shared fairly broadly with those affected both to validate them and to ensure understanding and acceptance.

Communication does not stop with the presentation of the plan. The need for continued communication on the plan and its progress is discussed more fully in the next chapter.

RESOURCES

Like other functions, communication pieces—particularly written ones—require resources. With the advent of the personal computer, desktop publishing and graphics software packages, many libraries now have the capability to produce good-looking communication pieces at low cost. Libraries should remember, however, that professional designers command fees because they have experience and expertise in strengthening the communication of a message through an effective design.

A budget for communication resources should include staff time, design costs, reproduction costs and distribution or mailing costs. Some libraries may already have some or all of these resources, while other libraries may need to use an outside firm. Vehicles for communicating the plan throughout its development and implementation include: press releases, newsletter articles, interviews with planning team participants or celebrity clientele, and brochures summarizing the plan. In addition, public libraries may want to enlist radio or television support.

The kinds of tools used, the ways of reaching the audience, the amount of information to be conveyed, and the frequency of conveying it will determine the amount of resources required. In this area, a library has a great deal of discretion. The library should always remember, however, that a well-constructed communication program can enhance acceptance and support of the strategic plan.

SUMMARY

Continued and effective communication is essential for the success of the strategic planning process. Communication should begin when the planning effort starts and should continue throughout the process. From the inception of the process through its implementation, effective communication tools can promote the input the plan will need from users, advisory groups, staff, boards and institutional officers. Moreover, input helps the library secure both a commitment from people to support implementation of the plan and the resources needed to implement it. Managers and planners should target communication tools to their audience. All communication should carry an appropriate message in a format and medium suited both to the message and the audience. The communications should be produced regularly. Resources for communication should be considered an integral part of the resources needed for planning. Communication is not an area to skimp on, since judicious investment in good communication tools can provide handsome returns by ensuring support for planning activities and by providing access to the necessary resources.

10 MONITORING AND EVALUATING

Plan Monitoring
   Plan Goals and Adjustments
   Individual Performance Goals and Review
   Cost Analysis
Monitoring the Environment
Summary

Establishing a vision, converting it into a mission statement, supporting it with goals, objectives, and action plans, writing and communicating the results of the planning progress are important. However, all of the activities involved in creating the strategic plan will not succeed unless the managers and planners carefully monitor the implementation of the plan. This stage consists of two related, but different activities: directly measuring the progress of the plan itself and continuing to monitor changes in the environment and underlying assumptions.

PLAN MONITORING

Part of the process of creating the objectives and the action plans requires the identification of measurable items or milestones. These milestones form the heart of the monitoring process. Each action plan contains specifics as to who performs the task (task responsibilities), what the task is and what the results of completing the task are (task definition and milestones), when the task is to be performed (schedules), where the task is to be performed, and how the task is to be performed. The results (products or services) are the items monitored and the milestone schedules with the personnel assigned to the task providing the keys to follow-up.

In the sixties, project planning systems were used to monitor the development of weapon systems, large-scale construction projects and computer systems software projects. Computers made such systems manageable and easier to update. More recently, project planning systems have become available for personal computers. As a result, such systems are now available to any manager with access to the necessary hardware. For large libraries, these systems can be useful in tracking progress on strategic plans or other projects. However, for small institutions, paper charts and tables usually will suffice.

Regardless of which tools a manager or planner uses to monitor progress, it is important that management use the plan, associated schedules, milestones and staff assignments to manage and to ensure that if progress is delayed appropriate actions are taken. A plan that sits on a shelf and is not an integral part of daily management is nothing more than a paperweight. To be effective a plan must guide daily decision making in the library. The library's progress in implementing the plan must be monitored and man-

Monitoring the Plan

Step 1
Measure the progress of the plan

Step 2
Monitor changes in the environment

aged, and both staff and the communities the library serves must be kept informed.

Two important areas that the strategic plan should guide are unit goals and individual performance. Whether or not a library uses management by objectives (MBO), the library should link individual performance goals to strategic planning goals. While some library systems are more restrictive than others, almost all include some provision for evaluation and for merit increases. Library managers must use these tools to achieve the library's overall goals. The manager should measure each staff member's individual performance in relation to strategic planning goals and the specific action plan tasks each staff member was assigned. Unless reward and performance evaluation systems are tied to these goals, staff will have little incentive to achieve them. It should be stressed, however, that progress primarily results from participation in plan development and associated commitment, but reinforcement through performance evaluation and reward systems is helpful.

Statistical and cost data from the library's operation should be part of the monitoring process. Such data can validate and refine any conceptual or computer models used such as those discussed in Chapter 8. Deciding on appropriate measures and implementing them are critical to the successful operation of the library. For example: Can an additional 1000 titles per year be processed with one added staff member? Can circulation queues be kept to five people or smaller during peak usage? There is no excuse for not knowing the operating costs of the library. In *The Bottom Line*, Jacob[1] provides a simple method for calculating costs as does Sager[2] in his guide to library automation planning.

A library manager should at least know costs for the following: salaries for each group, materials and supplies and maintenance and contracts. Moreover, a manager should know what each unit produces in measurable units (e.g., reference questions answered or books acquired, cataloged or processed). Unit costs can be calculated by dividing total recurring costs by total units produced. More sophisticated methods may involve diary studies, random sampling or survey methods. Parent institution cost accountants can advise on allocating overhead costs such as building space, utilities, senior administration salaries and other relevant items. Usually they are apportioned on either the amount of the space or time used, or on activity level. Where a manager knows equipment costs, they should also be included. The manager should prorate them over their anticipated useful life (i.e., total cost divided by expected life in years provides an annual cost). If library managers feel unable to apply techniques such as those described by Gherman[3] and Rosenberg,[4] they should seek the assistance of either outside consultants or their cost accounting colleagues within the parent institution. Figure 10-1 provides a simple example.

It is not important to calculate or determine exact costs down to the last penny, but to establish a relative level of cost and how it changes over time. Managers may also be interested in how their library's costs compare to the costs of institutions of similar size and type in a similar geographic area. Such an analysis is helpful in determining whether a library is becoming more or less efficient in its use of resources.

It is also important to note that a library must pay for time spent in meetings and on coffee breaks. Consequently, a library must factor these expenses into total costs. Even if staff could process more items in a given period, the real cost is based on the number of items actually processed, not a theoretical maximum number of items. Managers should know their unit costs and the productivity of their staff.

Recent papers presented to the International Federation of Library Associations (IFLA) Statistics and University Libraries Sections have been devoted to performance measures including Walters,[5] Ford,[6] and Willemse.[7] The literature on this topic continues to grow.

In 1987, OCLC surveyed it member libraries on their planning practices.[8] While more libraries are planning, the OCLC survey showed that few of them are using monitoring and evaluation techniques to review and manage the progress on the planning activities. Without this controlling feedback, however, planning is an empty process.

MONITORING THE ENVIRONMENT

The second aspect of monitoring relates to changes in the environment. As noted in Chapter 3, the environmental review process is ongoing. At periodic points, such as quarterly, semi-annually, or annually, the planner or manager should monitor changes in the library's environment. The objective is to identify changes and to assess the impact of change on the plan and plan assumptions. Depending on the timeframe and the type of environmental change,

FIGURE 10-1 GROSS UNIT COST EXAMPLE

$$\text{Unit costs} = \frac{\text{Total recurring costs} + \text{Prorated fixed costs}}{\text{Units processed}}$$

Total recurring costs:
    Salaries of staff performing the function being costed
    Benefits of staff performing the function being costed
    Supplies used for this function
    Contractual or maintenance costs for the function
    Rental costs of equipment used for the function
    Materials costs for the function (book or journal
        costs, subscription fees)
    Services (online search costs, record use charges,
        telecommunications related to this function)

Prorated fixed costs
    Overhead (administration, space, utilities)
    Equipment costs (total cost/useful life)

Units processed (use whichever applies to function being costed)
(the categories below are illustrative and not exhaustive)
    Items cataloged or processed
    Reference questions answered
    Reference searches performed
    Serial issues checked in
    Items circulated

Note: all cost figures must be for the same period of time, i.e. weekly, monthly or yearly, and units processed must represent the same time period. Normal practice is to use annual figures since vacation and sick leave would normally even out over a full year but might create anomalies in weekly or even monthly reports.

The numerator for circulation unit costs would include the salaries of circulation staff and their benefits, any allocation for space, furnishings and utilities and that portion of an automated system used to support circulation, equipment maintenance, contract service and supplies. While the average book costs could be included, normally such costs are allocated to collection building or acquisitions functions. The number of items circulated would be the denominator.

the plan may require little or no change. Environmental change is more likely to affect specific action plans than any other part of the plan. If the planning process has been well done, the library will already have assessed the likely impact of potential changes and therefore will have identified a suitable course of action. If something unforeseen occurs, then the planning team should redo its scenarios and assess the various possible repercussions. The team can then chose the best course of action. At this point, the planning process has come full circle, and the team will repeat those parts of the cycle as needed and revise the plan as required.

SUMMARY

Successful implementation of the library's strategic plan requires continuous monitoring and evaluation of the plan process. In addition, it requires continuous monitoring and evaluation of the environment. Planning without monitoring and evaluation is wishful thinking, not true planning. The team and managers must monitor the library's progress towards its goals and the impact of environmental changes on its mission and goals. In the event milestones are not met or major environmental changes occur which could potentially affect one or more goals, the team and management must take appropriate action. Individual performance measurement can be a powerful tool when it is used to ensure adherence to plan objectives. Other important tools include plan schedules and a thorough knowledge of library costs and productivity. Communication of plan progress to staff, users and institutional officers is essential. Making strategic planning and strategic management work is an active, participative process.

REFERENCES

1. M.E.L. Jacob, "Costing and Pricing: the Difference Matters," *Bottom Line*, 2(2) (1988):12-14.
2. Donald J. Sager, *Public Library Administrators' Planning Guide to Automation* (Dublin, Ohio: OCLC, 1983). 0-933418-43-4.
3. Paul Gherman and Lynn Scott Cochrane, "Developing and Using Unit Cost: the Virginia Tech Experience," *LAMA* 3(2) (Spring 1989):93-96.

4. Phillip Rosenberg, *Costing for Public Libraries: a Manager's Handbook,* (Chicago: American Library Association, 1985).
5. Clarence Walters, "The Use of Performance Measures by Public Libraries in the United States," IFLA Statistics Section Paper (Sydney, 1988).
6. Geoffrey Ford, "Performance Measurement: Principles and Practices," IFLA Statistics Section Paper. (Sydney, 1988).
7. John Willemse, "Library Effectiveness—the Need for Measurement," IFLA University Libraries Section Paper (Sydney, 1988).
8. M.E.L. Jacob, *Planning in OCLC Member Libraries,* ed. asst. Sondra Albanese, *OCLC Library, Information, and Computer Science Series,* 9 (Dublin, Ohio: OCLC, 1988). 1-55653-051-X.

11 END NOTE

This manual has set forth a step-by-step explanation of the strategic planning process. Each chapter has included samples and workforms to help create a strategic plan. A checklist appears in Figure 11-1. Readers should have answers to all the questions posed in the final version of their plan. If they do not, they should review the manual and the plan in that section and other sections as needed and make the necessary revisions. Revisions in assumptions, vision, mission, or goals require revisions throughout the entire plan, whereas revisions in a specific action plan may or may not affect other parts of the plan.

What are the pitfalls? Although some of these were discussed in previous chapters, a summary of the pitfalls follows:

> Unrealistic or overly ambitious goals not firmly based on fact
> Unrealistic or inaccurate assumptions
> Failure to fully document and share assumptions
> Failure to involve and gain the commitment of those required to implement the plan
> Lack of leadership and follow-up
> Lack of a monitoring and evaluation process including a maintenance process for the plan
> Failure to align performance review and reward systems with plan goals
> Failure to align library procedures and policies with plan
> Failure to link plan with institutional goals
> Failure to acquire adequate resources to implement plan
> Failure to communicate fully and accurately with staff, clientele, funders and administrative authorities
> Failure to understand and use the political processes affecting the library
> Lack of creativity and goals with sufficient reach to move the library into a leadership role
> Inertia and fear of change (it is easier to accept the status quo even when that means diminished resources).

With energy, enthusiasm, commitment and leadership all of these pitfalls can be surmounted. The miracles promised in Chapter 1 can be achieved. A library can visualize a future and make that future happen. It requires hard work, but it is possible. This guide has already given readers the tools to avoid these pitfalls. If they follow it, they should be able to overcome all of them.

The keys are interaction, participation and constant communication. There should be no surprises when the team has completed the plan. The results should seem inevitable, a natural outgrowth

FIGURE 11-1 STRATEGIC PLANNING CHECKLIST

ASSUMPTIONS
- Are they written?
- Are they complete?
- Are they realistic?

ENVIRONMENTAL SCAN
- Have all relevant factors been considered?
- Have trends and implications been explicitly identified?
- Have "what if" scenarios been developed?
- Have threats and opportunities been evaluated?

VISION
- What does the library want to be in 5 years, 10 years?
- What is needed to make this happen?
- Is it achievable?

MISSION
- Who does the library serve?
- What are their needs?
- How does the library meet the needs of these groups?
- What are a library's values?

GOALS
- Are these broad, long-term statements?
- Do they provide amplification and focus to the mission?
- Are they program oriented (as opposed to task oriented)?

OBJECTIVES
- Are these specific, measurable and time-limited?
- Do they support both the mission and the broad goals?

ACTION PLANS
- What is the task to be done in support of specific objectives?
- How is the task to be accomplished?
- Who is to do it?
- When is it to be started and completed?
- Does it have measurable milestones and results?
- Do you know when you are finished?
- What is the tangible result of the action?
- Have resources been identified and are they available?

CONTINGENCIES
- Have "what if" scenarios been prepared and optional strategies considered?
- Are these realistic courses of action?
- What is the likelihood of such events occurring?

FIGURE 11-1 *Continued*

POLICIES
- Has the library/institution prepared written operating policies?
- Will new policies be needed because of the proposed plan?
- Are existing policies and procedures compatible with and supportive of the plan?

RESOURCE ALLOCATION
- Have supporting resource requirements been prepared to support the plan?
- Are resources available or can they be acquired?
- Are the resource estimates realistic?
- Is the plan used to develop annual or other budgets?

MONITORING AND EVALUATION
- Does a plan exist for monitoring and evaluating the progress of the plan?
- Who is responsible for monitoring and evaluation?
- When and how is monitoring and evaluation done?
- Are the results of monitoring and evaluation used to update the plan?
- Is the monitoring and evaluation process linked to the performance and review process for staff?

PLAN FORMAT AND COMMUNICATION
- Has a communication plan been prepared?
- Have the various audiences to be communicated with been defined?
- Is the content and format consistent with the audience and the information to be communicated?
- Are the resources needed available?

of the library's response to environmental trends and the creation of a shared vision.

Ideally, users, institutional management, library management and staff have participated in all phases of the planning process. They are not only aware of what has been learned in the process, they also know how library management and planners are using that learning to shape the best future for the library. Following the planning process ensures that a realistic plan has been developed and implemented. Library management and staff must continue to monitor the plan's progress and any environmental changes that may affect it. They must fine tune the plan as needed. The management and staff are managing the plan; the plan is not managing them. The plan is providing a framework for enhanced communication, productivity and decision making.

The benefits of planning are many. A few include:

> Meeting the primary needs of clientele
> Better resource management, use and allocation
> More effective resource procurement
> Consistent decentralized decision making
> Consensus and commitment on the library's future
> Ability to more readily understand how changes in the environment will affect the library
> Proactive leadership role, instead of passive, follower role
> Better positioning within parent institution.

Surely these benefits make all the effort worthwhile!

APPENDIX A.
Market Research Firms

The Caroll Group
875 N. Michigan Ave.
Suite 3311
Chicago, IL 60611

The Competitor Intelligence Group
2021 Midwest Road
Suite 300
Oak Brook, IL 60521

Marketing Audit
1524 Pine Street
Philadelphia, PA 19102

M.E.L. Jacob Associates
3787 Patricia Drive
Columbus, OH 43220

Special Information Services
7212 13th Ave
Washington, D.C. 20012

Strategic Intelligence Systems, Inc
404 Park Ave, South
Suite 1301
New York, NY 10016

APPENDIX B.
Library Futures

Adams, Roy J. *Information Technology and Libraries: a Future for Academic Libraries.* London: Croom Helm, 1986.

Cummings, Martin Marc, ed. *Influencing Change in Research Librarianship: a Festschrift for Warren J. Haas.* Washington, D.C.: Council for Library Resources, 1988.

Hayes, Robert M., ed. *Universities, Information Technology, and Academic Libraries: the Next Twenty Years.* Norwood, New Jersey: Ablex, 1986.

Matheson, Nina and John A.D. Cooper. "Academic Information in the Academic Health Sciences Center: Roles for the Library in Information Management." *Journal of Medical Education* 57(10), part 2, October 1982.

Shuman, Bruce. *The Library of the Future: Alternative Scenarios for the Information Profession.* Englewood, Colorado: Libraries Unlimited, 1989.

Taylor, Betty W., Elizabeth B. Mann and Robert J. Munro. *The Twenty-first Century: Technology's Impact on Academic Research and Law Libraries.* Boston: G.K. Hall, 1988.

Walters, Clarence R., ed. *The Future of the Public Library: Conference Proceedings.* Dublin, Ohio: OCLC, 1988.

Webster, Duane, et al. "Organizational Projections for Assessing Future Research Library Staffing Needs and Processes." *Organizational Futures: Staffing Research Libraries in the 1990s.* Minutes of the 105th Meeting, October 24-29, 1984. Washington, D.C.: ARL, 1985: 6-15.

Williams, Martha E. "ASIS 2000: an open forum for the 1990s." *ASIS Bulletin* 16(1) October/November 1989:8-29.

STRATEGIC PLANNING GLOSSARY

Action plans: Plans incorporating statements of who, what, how, when, and where specific tasks are to be completed. A list of specific milestones or measurable points of progress should be included. The needs for action are defined by the institution's mission, goals, and objectives.

Assumptions: All planning contains certain assumptions about an institution and its environment. It is essential that these be stated explicitly and monitored against the environment for possible change.

Contingent strategies: Strategies which may be used in place of primary strategies because of environmental change.

Environmental scanning: A formal ongoing process of monitoring the environment and assessing the impact of various trends on an institution.

Goals: Broad statements identifying long-range objectives and activities an organization plans to pursue.

Linkage: The process of ensuring that the library or unit plan is linked with and supportive of the parent organization's plan, mission, goals, and objectives.

Measurability: Quantifying or identifying some method of determining whether a specific goal or objective has been achieved. Normally if all the objectives under a goal have been achieved, the goal has been achieved unless the objectives identified were insufficient to the achievement of the entire goal.

Mission statement: Broad definition of an institution and its focus, which should identify its sphere of influence, its clientele, and major activity focus.

Modeling: Process of creating a meta-representation of a process, service, function, or activity. This may be conceptual, a spreadsheet, or other computer manipulable representation.

Monitoring: Process of reviewing measurable results and progress of the plan and ensuring that action plans are completed and taking action as needed to maintain schedules.

Objectives: Specific measurable and time-limited actions or activities in support of goal statements.

Opportunities: May be created by environmental trends or threats when viewed from a different perspective.

Performance review: Reviewing staff performance and ensuring it is in line with and supportive of strategic planning objectives.

Planning cycle: Cycle of planning and revision. Usually strategic plans cover a five-year cycle and are revised annually.

Planning process: The steps and actions required to create a functional strategic plan. The planning process is continual.

Policies: Those formal principles, procedures, assumptions, and practices that govern how an institution operates. These should be consistent with and supportive of an institution's mission and strategic plan.

Priorities: Establish the sequence and precedence of goals, objectives, and activities to best fulfill an institution's mission.

Resource allocation: Process of identifying, acquiring, prioritizing, and assigning all the needed resources including staff, expertise, equipment, materials, funding, etc., to complete specific actions.

Scenarios: "What if" descriptions of the environment given different assumptions or outcomes of certain actions.

Strategic Planning: Identifying and implementing from among many the most appropriate course of action that will best achieve an institution's vision of what it is and what it should be. Identifying current decisions that will create a desired future.

Strategies: A means of achieving specific objectives or carrying out specific activities.

Strengths: Those characteristics that an institution has that make it better able than others to achieve certain of its goals and objectives.

Tactics: The short-term action plans required to implement the strategic plan.

Threats: Conditions in the environment usually created by others that can interfere with an institution's plans, survival, or welfare. When viewed from a different framework, threats become opportunities.

Value: The worth assigned by a particular individual to goods, services, or properties. Different participants will have different value systems.

Value-added: The process of adding value to goods, services, or property.

Vision: A statement of the future desired state of an institution or unit usually representing an improvement over its current state and requiring the application of resources and actions to achieve.

Weaknesses: Those characteristics or conditions that work against or prevent an institution from achieving its goals and objectives

BIBLIOGRAPHY

American Library Association. *Planning and Role Setting for Public Libraries: A Manual of Options and Procedures.* Chicago: ALA, 1987.

Arterbery, Vivian J. "SLA's Long-Range Planning: A Vision for the Future." *Special Libraries.* Washington, D.C.: Special Libraries Association, 1984. 75:61-68.

Association of College and Research Libraries. *ACRL's Strategic Plan.* Chicago: ACRL, 1987.

Association of Research Libraries. *Strategic Planning in ARL Libraries,* ARL SPEC Kit No. 108. Washington DC: ARL Office of Management Studies, 1984.

Bolt, Nancy and Corine Johnson. *Options for Small Libraries in Massachusetts: Recommendations and a Planning Guide.* Chicago: American Library Association, 1985.

Campbell, William D. *A Budgeting Manual for Small Public Libraries.* Clarion, Pennsylvania: College of Library Science, Clarion University of Pennsylvania, Center for the Study of Rural Librarianship and the Small Library Development Center, 1987.

Drucker, Peter Ferdinand. *Management: Tasks, Responsibilities, Practices.* New York: Harper & Row, 1974.

Gardner, David Morgan. *Strategic Planning.* Videorecording. VHS, 57 minutes. Dublin, Ohio: OCLC Users Council, 1985.

Gardner, Jeffrey. *Resource Notebook on Planning.* Washington, D.C.: Office of Management Statistics. Association of Research Libraries, 1979.

Hyatt, James A. *University Libraries in Transition.* Washington, D.C.: National Association of College and University Business Officers (NACUBO), 1987.

Louisiana State Library. 1972. *Clear Purpose, Complete Commitment.* Baton Rouge: LSL.

Massachusetts Board of Library Commissioners. *Automated Resource Sharing in Massachusetts: A Plan.* Boston: Commonwealth of Massachusetts, 1983.

Massachusetts Board of Library Commissioners. *Long Range Program, 1987-1991.* Boston: Commonwealth of Massachusetts, 1986.

Matheson, Nina W., and John A.D. Cooper. "Academic Information in the Academic Health Sciences Center: Roles for the Library in Information Management." *Journal of Medical Education.* (1982) 57:1-93.

McClure, Charles R. "Library Planning: A Status Report." *ALA Yearbook of Library and Information Services.* Chicago: American Library Association, 1986.

McClure, Charles R. et al. *Planning and Role Setting for Public Libraries.* Chicago: American Library Association, 1987.

Medical Library Association. *Shaping the Future: The Strategic Plan of the Medical Library Association.* Chicago: MLA, 1987.

Molz, R. Kathleen. *National Planning for Library Service 1935-1975.* Chicago: American Library Association, 1984.

National Library of Medicine. *Long Range Plan.* Washington, D.C.: U.S. Department of Health and Human Services, 1986-87.

Nolan, Timothy M. *Applied Strategic Planning in a Library Setting.* San Diego: University Associates, 1987.

O'Donnell, Peggy. *Public Library Development Program: Manual for Trainers.* Chicago: American Library Association, 1988.

Online Computer Library Center, Inc. *Campus of the Future: Conference on Information Resources.* Dublin, Ohio: OCLC, 1986.

Palmour, Vernon E. *A Planning Process for Public Libraries.* Chicago: American Library Association, 1980.

Pfeiffer, J. William and Leonard D. Goodstein and Timothy M. Nolan. *Shaping Strategic Planning: Frogs, Dragons, Bees, and Turkey Tails.* Glenview, Illinois: Scott, Foresman, 1989.

Ramsey, Inez, and Jackson E. Ramsey. *Library Planning and Budgeting.* New York: Franklin Watts, Inc., 1986

Riggs, Donald E. *Strategic Planning for Library Managers.* Phoenix: Oryx Press, 1984.

Sager, Donald J. *Public Library Administrators' Planning Guide to Automation.* Dublin, Ohio: OCLC, 1983.

Stubbs, Kendon Lee. *Quantitative Criteria for Academic Research Libraries.* Chicago: Association of College and Research Libraries, American Library Association, 1984.

University of the State of New York, State Education Department. *Library Service to the People of New York State: A Long-Range Program.* Albany: New York, March 1987.

Van House, Nancy A. et al. *Output Measures for Public Libraries: A Manual of Standardized Procedures.* Chicago and London: American Library Association, 1987.

Virgo, Julie A.C. *Principles of Strategic Planning in the Library Environment.* Chicago: Association of College and Research Libraries, 1984.

INDEX

Academic libraries, 4, 6, 7, 8, 28, 50, 63
Accreditation, 8, 20, 54

Action Plans, 61, 67, 73, 91, 101, 102
Advisory Bodies, 10, 26-28, 58, 89, 99
Agricola, 81
Allocation, see Resource allocation
Alternative actions, 31, 53-54, 82-85
American Library Association, 6, 7, 8, 60, 106
Anderson, James, 75, 86
ARL, see Association of Research Libraries
ARL Spec Kit #108, 8
Association of Research Libraries, 7, 8, 46-47
Assumptions, 9, 12, 21, 25, 31-37, 39, 40, 53-54, 61, 83-85, 91, 98, 101, 103, 107
AT&T Bell Laboratories, 93
Audiences, 89-93

Batelle Memorial Institute, 46, 47
Blue Ribbon panels, 58
Bolt, Nancy, 6, 8, 53, 60
Bottom Line, 75, 86, 102, 105
Boucher, Wayne, 60
Brainstorming, 11, 33
Brochures, 7, 11, 28, 93, 97, 99
Budgets, 20, 22, 27, 54, 75, 76, 85-86, 98-99

California, 4, 6, 58, 83
Celebrities, 79, 98
Chamber of Commerce, 26, 50
Chief Officers of State Library Agencies, 7
Clark, Philip, 83, 86
Clientele, 1, 21, 55-58, 75, 85, 89, 97-98, 107, see also Users
Coca-Cola, 79

Collections, 12, 21, 63
Commissions on the Future, 50
Commitment, 2, 9-13, 23, 99, 107-110
Communication, 11-12, 13, 15, 23, 34, 89-99, 105, 107-110
Communities, 12-13, 15, 25-29, 34, 53, 55-58, 61, 63, 82, 85, 89, 97, 102
Community Assessment, 12-13, 58
Competition, 31, 34, 58-59
Constraints, 31-34, 79, see also Obstacles
Consultants, 20, 22, 23, 47, 50, 98, 103
Contingency plans, see Alternative actions
Contractors, 20, see also Consultants
Cooper, John A.D., 8
Corporate libraries, 10, 28, 32, 50, 63
COSLA, 7
Costs, 22, 53, 58, 59, 83-85, 98-99, 102-103

Data gathering, 14, 23, 31-37, 39-60
Decision-making, 9, 23, 83
Demographics, 4, 32, 39
Donors, 32, 85
Drucker, Peter, 9, 24

Eaton, Nancy, 6
Enrollments, 4, 39
Environmental assessment, 12, 14-15, 21, 39-60, 103-105
Environmental scanning, 7, 12, 21, 31, 39-60, 103-105
Environmental trends, 1, 14, 21-22, 39-60, 91, 98, 103-105
Environmental tracking, see Environmental scanning
ERIC, 81
Ethics, 64

Evaluation, 101-106

Faculties, 10, 25-26, 63, 72
Florida, 6
Forecasts, 3, 46, 47, see also Environmental Assessment, Environmental scanning, Environmental trends
Ford, Geoffrey, 103, 106
Format (Plan), 89-93
Friends, 32
Funding, 4, 32, 83, 85-86
Futures, 39-54, see also Environmental trends, Scenarios

Gherman, Paul, 59, 60, 103, 105
Goals, 2, 7, 13, 15, 25, 32, 53, 55, 64-65, 72, 73, 85-86, 89-91, 97, 101-102, 105, 107
Goodstein, Leonard D., 60
Governance, 9, see also Advisory bodies
GPO, see U.S. Government Printing Office
Graphics, 92-93, 98
Gutlick, Luther, 1, 2

Harvard University, 3, 8
Heydinger, Richard, 46, 60

IAIMS, 5
IFLA, see International Federation of Library Associations
IIA, see Information Industry Association
Implementation, 11-12, 23, 34, 89-99, 101-106
Information Industry Association, 46
Institution, 1-2, 5, 9, 10, 12-15, 20, 21, 23, 25-29, 31-32, 39, 48, 54-55, 72,

INDEX

Institution, (*Continued*)
    75-77, 85-86, 89-91, 97, 107
Institutional assessment, 54-55
Integrated Automated Information Management System, 5
International Federation of Library Associations, 103, 106

Jacob, M.E.L., 9, 75, 83, 86, 102, 105, 106
Johnson, Corine, 6, 9, 53, 60

Las Vegas-Clark County Public Library, 93
LC, *see* Library of Congress
Leadership, 2, 9, 107-110
Leaflets, 11, 28, 93, 97
Library Assessment, 14-15, 21, 55-59
Library of Congress, 5, 79
Library Services and Construction Act, 5, 6
Licensing, 79
Linkage, 25-29
Lotus, 13, 87
LSCA, 5, 6

Machalow, Robert, 83, 87
Maintenance, *see* Updating
MARC, 5, 79
Massachusetts, 4, 6, 8, 53, 60
Matheson, Nina, 5, 8
McClure, Charles, 8, 60
Medical Library Association, 7
Milestones, 67, 73, 93, 101, 105
Mission, 27, 53, 55, 58, 61-73, 89-91, 98, 101, 107
Models, 13-15, 23, 31, 34, 59, 77, 79, 83-85, 102
Monitoring, 15, 91, 97, 101-106, 107-110

National Agriculture Library, 6

National Commission on Libraries and Information Science, 5
National Library of Medicine, 5-6, 8
National Technical Information Service, 80
NCLIS, 5
Networks, 5, 6, 7, 28, 32
Newsletters, 11, 28, 97-98
Newspapers, 26, 28, 98
NLM, 5-6, 8
Nominal small groups, 33

Objectives, 1-2, 20, 29, 53, 55, 58, 61, 64-67, 74-83, 89-91, 97, 101-102
Obstacles, 1, 31, 32, 107
OCLC, 7, 8, 39, 47, 81, 86, 93, 103, 106
Ohio State University, 6
Opportunities, 21, 31-32, 34, 59, 91
Ownership of information, 46, 77-79
Ownership of strategic plan, 11

Participation, 9-13, 21, 25-29, 102
Pepsi, 79
Performance and reward systems, 4, 72, 101-102, 107
Pfeiffer, William J., 46, 60
PLA, *see* Public Library Association
Plan format, 89-93
Planning objectives, 20
Planning process model, 13-15
Planning rationale, 20, 91
Planning team, 11, 15-23
Policies, 10, 72, 102
Porter, Michael, 4, 8, 31
PPB, 3
Priorities, 82-86
Procedures, *see* Policies
Productivity, 59, 83-85, 102-103
Proposition 2½, 4

Proposition 13, 4, 58
Public Libraries, 9, 26, 28, 32, 50, 52-53, 60, 63, 99, 106
Public Library Association, 6-7, 52

Renfro, William L., 60
Research Libraries Group, 7
Resource allocation, 1, 10, 27, 32, 50, 53, 54, 58, 75-87, 107-110
RLG, 7
Roberts, Stephen A., 59, 60
Rosenberg, Philip, 59, 60, 103, 106

Sager, Donald, 102, 105
Scanning, *see* Environmental scanning
Scenarios, 39-47, 53-54, 86, 91
Schauer, Bruce P., 75, 86
Schedules, 22-23, 65-67, 98, 101, 103, 105
Scott, Lynn Cochrane, 60, 105
Simulation, *see* Models
Situation analysis, *see* Environmental assessment, Institution assessment, Library assessment
SLA, *see* Special Libraries Association
Software, 13, 23, 83, 86-87, 93, 101
Special Libraries, *see* Corporate Libraries
Special Libraries Association, 7, 47
Spreadsheet, 13, 83, 86-87
Statistics, 102, *see also* Data gathering, Surveys
Strategic management, 1-2
Strategic planning (definition), 1-2
Strategic planning process, 9-24
Strengths, 14-15, 21, 29, 55, 59, 91
Strong, Gary, 6
Supercalc, 13

Surveys, 20, 21, 23, 52-53

Tactics, 2
Task groups, 11, 15, 21
Tax, 77
Taylor, Robert S., 75, 79, 81, 86
Teams, *see* Planning team, Task groups
Technology, 4, 39, 47, 53, 86
Threats, 21, 58, 91

Updating, 12, 15, 103-105, 107
Urwick, Lydall, 2
USAIN, 6

Users, 10, 12, 25-29, 34, 50, 53, 55, 58, 75, 89, 97, 99, 105, 110
U.S. Census Bureau, 50
U.S. Government Printing Office, 80
U.S. Office of Education, 5, 6

Validation, 32-33, 102-103
Value-added services, 75, 77-82
Value-added tax, 77
Values, 63-64, 75-77, 82-83, 85-86
Vancil, Richard, 8
VAT, 77
Virginia Tech, 60, 105

Vision, 1, 9, 11, 13, 25, 60, 61, 64, 82, 89, 101, 107-110

Walters, Clarence, 103, 106
Weaknesses, 14-15, 21, 55, 59, 91
Webster, Dwayne, 47
Western Library Network, 7
White House Conference, 1979, 5
Wilkins, Barrett, 6
Willemse, John, 103, 106
WLN, *see* Western Library Network

Zaltmon, Gerald, 1, 2
Zentner, Rene, 46, 60